Reader's Guide to Scotland

A BIBLIOGRAPHY

1968

THE NATIONAL BOOK LEAGUE
7 ALBEMARLE STREET
LONDON W1

SBN 85353 012 2

First published 1968

Set in 10 on 11 pt Scotch Roman

Printed in Great Britain by
W & J Mackay & Co Ltd, Chatham

CONTENTS

INTRODUCTION

This list in its main outlines follows the plan of that of 1950, compiled by the late Dr Henry W. Meikle and his collaborators, a list which is one of the main sources for the present one. The editor of this second list, D. M. Lloyd, Keeper of Printed Books, National Library of Scotland, is, in the last resort, responsible for the arrangement and final selection of the items. The arrangement and almost the whole of the selection, however, of Section II—History, was made by Dr T. I. Rae, M.A., Ph.D., Assistant Keeper in the Department of Manuscripts in that Library.

Where no price is given, the book, at the time of compilation, was out of print, and thanks are due to Mr James Thin for supplying information on this point. Most of the out-of-print books mentioned are accessible in public libraries and, if not available locally, can be sought for through the Scottish Central Library. Many of them can also be bought second-hand.

With a very few exceptions, a book which bears on two or more different subjects is listed only in the section which appears to be most appropriate. 'London' is omitted from the imprint in the case of books published there.

Much valuable information and guidance have been obtained from various Government departments, institutions and experts whose help is gratefully acknowledged. They include those mentioned below. The editor also owes a great deal in advice and assistance to Professor William Beattie, C.B.E., LL.D., Litt.D., Librarian of the National Library of Scotland, and to several members of the staff, but particularly to Miss Margaret Johnston, M.A., Miss M. P. Linton, M.A., (Deputy Keepers of Printed Books) and M. A. Begg, Esq., M.A., Assistant Keeper.

Information and guidance was received from various Departments of the Secretary of State for Scotland through the good offices of W. M. Ballantine Esq., C.B.E., M.V.O., of the Scottish Information Office. Other helpers include D. K. Baxandall, Esq., C.B.E., B.A., F.M.A., Dr George Davie, M.A., D. Litt., Ian Finlay, Esq., C.B.E., M.A., Professor C. J. Fordyce, M.A., LL.D., Charles Graves, Esq., Hamish Henderson, Esq., M.A., Miss F. Marion McNeill, M.B.E., M.A., Professor John MacQueen, M.A., Rev. W.

Matheson, M.A., D. D. Murison, Esq., M.A., B.A., W. F. H. Nicolaisen, Esq., Dr. Phil., B. Litt., F.S.A. (Scot.), Alexander Rodger, Esq., M.A., Professor T. B. Smith, Q.C., M.A., D.C.L., LL.D., F.B.A., W. A. Thorburn, Esq., (Curator, Scottish United Services Museum).

1 General

Ballantine, W. M. SCOTLAND NOW. *H.M.S.O.* (*Scottish Development Department*) 1960, 3*s*.

Finlay, Ian. SCOTLAND. *Chatto & Windus* 1957.

Foreman, J. B., *general ed.* SCOTLAND'S SPLENDOUR AS SEEN BY GEORGE BLAKE AND OTHERS. *Glasgow, Collins* 1960, 35*s*.
Richly illustrated in colour.

Sissons, J. B. THE EVOLUTION OF SCOTLAND'S SCENERY. *Edinburgh, Oliver & Boyd* 1967, 63*s*.

Maine, G. F., *ed.* A BOOK OF SCOTLAND. *Collins* 1950, 16*s*.
An anthology of prose and verse and comments on Scottish life and character.

Meikle, H. W., *ed.* SCOTLAND: a description of Scotland and Scottish life. *Edinburgh, Nelson* 1947.
Thirty-two chapters by experts on various aspects of Scottish life.

Muir, Augustus. SCOTTISH PORTRAIT. *Edinburgh, Hopetoun Press* 1948.

Royal Commission on Scottish Affairs. REPORT, 1952–54. *Edinburgh, H.M.S.O.* (*Cmd. 9212*) 1954, 4*s*.

Also available, MINUTES OF EVIDENCE, 1953–54 in 10 parts, and MEMORANDA SUBMITTED TO THE COMMISSION, 1953 in 4 vols., at various prices.

Scottish Council (Development and Industry). INQUIRY INTO THE SCOTTISH ECONOMY, 1960–61, (The Toothill Report). *Edinburgh, H.M.S.O.* 1961.

Scottish Office. THE SCOTTISH ECONOMY, 1965–70: a plan for expansion. *H.M.S.O.* (*Cmnd. 2864*) 1966, 12*s* 6*d*.

Smith, Edwin, *photographer*. SCOTLAND; text by Eric Linklater. *Thames & Hudson* 1968, 63*s*.
Contains 134 photographic plates.

THE THIRD STATISTICAL ACCOUNT OF SCOTLAND. *Glasgow, Collins and Edinburgh, Oliver & Boyd* 1951.

To be completed in 28 vols. of which 17 have appeared to date, at various prices. Some published by *Collins* and some by *Oliver & Boyd*. The first STATISTICAL ACCOUNT was a survey of Scotland by parishes, ed. by Sir John Sinclair, *Edinburgh, W. Creech* 1791–99, 21 vols. and ANALYSIS, *John Murray* 1826. The second, THE NEW STATISTICAL ACCOUNT, *Edinburgh and London, Blackwood* 1845, 15 vols., is also arranged by parishes. These three surveys are unique sources for the history of all parts of Scotland, especially social and economic.

Wright, J. N. and Snodgrass, N. S., *eds*. SCOTLAND AND ITS PEOPLE: a symposium. *Edinburgh, Oliver & Boyd* 1942.

Essays by various authors on different aspects of Scottish life.

2 History

Although this list of books on Scottish history attempts to cover all aspects of the subject, it is, for reasons of space, highly selective. The emphasis is partly on books currently in print; but important standard works, and old works on subjects not recently reviewed by historians, are also included. The standard for selection of a book has largely been that of academic thoroughness in dealing with its subject. This has meant that a number of books on interesting topics, eminently readable though they are, have been omitted. No attempt has been made to guide the ordinary reader to the basic source material. Recent developments in historical studies are reported and reviewed in THE SCOTTISH HISTORICAL REVIEW, published twice yearly by the *Aberdeen University Press* for the *Company of Scottish History*.

I GENERAL WORKS

Brown, P. Hume. HISTORY OF SCOTLAND. 3 vols. *Cambridge University Press* 1900–9.
Detailed, straightforward account of political events.

Mackie, R. L. A SHORT HISTORY OF SCOTLAND. Rev. edn. by G. Donaldson. *Edinburgh, Oliver & Boyd* 1962, 21*s*.
First published in 1929.

Mackie, J. D. A HISTORY OF SCOTLAND. *Penguin* (*Pelican*) 1964, 6*s*.
The basic story in convenient form.

Dickinson, W. Croft and Pryde, G. S. A NEW HISTORY OF SCOTLAND. 2 vols. *Edinburgh, Nelson* 1961–2, 45*s* each.
Uses the results of more recent research, and takes a wider view of what constitutes the subject matter of history.

Donaldson, G. SCOTTISH KINGS. *Batsford* 1967, 35*s*.

Donaldson, G., *ed.* THE EDINBURGH HISTORY OF SCOTLAND. *Edinburgh, Oliver & Boyd.*
A series to be completed in four volumes, each by a separate author.
Vol. III. Donaldson, G. James V to James VII. 1965, 63*s*.

Vol. IV. Ferguson, W. Scotland: 1689 to the Present. 1968, 84*s*.

Burleigh, J. H. S. A CHURCH HISTORY OF SCOTLAND. *Oxford University Press* 1960, 42*s*.
The only complete history of the Church in Scotland.

II PREHISTORIC, ROMAN, AND DARK AGE SCOTLAND

Piggott, S., *ed.* THE PREHISTORIC PEOPLES OF SCOTLAND. *Routledge & Kegan Paul* 1962, 40*s*.
Puts the archaeological evidence into historical perspective.

Piggott, S. SCOTLAND BEFORE HISTORY. *Edinburgh, Nelson* 1958.
Attractive and non-technical with illustrations by Keith Henderson.

Lacaille, A. D. THE STONE AGE IN SCOTLAND. *Wellcome Historical Medical Library* 1954, 55*s*.

Childe, V. Gordon. SCOTLAND BEFORE THE SCOTS. *Methuen* 1946.

Childe, V. Gordon. THE PREHISTORY OF SCOTLAND. *Kegan Paul* 1935.

Feachem, R. W. A GUIDE TO PREHISTORIC SCOTLAND. *Batsford* 1963, 35*s*.
Lists the important archaeological sites.

Feachem, R. W. THE NORTH BRITONS: the prehistory of a border people. *Hutchinson* 1965, 45*s*.

Richmond, I. A., *ed.* ROMAN AND NATIVE IN NORTH BRITAIN. *Edinburgh, Nelson* 1958, 21*s*.
Best introduction to Roman occupation of Scotland.

Miller, S. N., *ed.* THE ROMAN OCCUPATION OF SOUTH-WESTERN SCOTLAND. *Glasgow, Maclehose* 1952.

Macdonald, *Sir* George. THE ROMAN WALL IN SCOTLAND. 2nd edn. *Oxford, Clarendon Press* 1934, 63*s*.

Simpson, W. Douglas. THE ANCIENT STONES OF SCOTLAND. 2nd edn. *Hale* 1968, 30*s*.

Crawford, O. G. S. TOPOGRAPHY OF ROMAN SCOTLAND NORTH OF THE ANTONINE WALL. *Cambridge University Press* 1949, 50*s*.

Henderson, Isabel. THE PICTS. *Thames & Hudson* 1967, 42*s*.

Wainwright, F. T., *ed.* THE PROBLEM OF THE PICTS. *Edinburgh, Nelson* 1955.

Wainwright, F. T., *ed.* THE NORTHERN ISLES. *Edinburgh, Nelson* 1962. 30*s*.

Chadwick, H. M. EARLY SCOTLAND. *Cambridge University Press* 1949.
Controversial.

III MEDIAEVAL SCOTLAND

(a) POLITICS AND ADMINISTRATION

Details of political affairs are given in studies of particular events and biographies of particular people; some of these studies go far beyond purely political affairs. There is as yet no comprehensive single work on Scottish mediaeval government. The best information can be obtained from introductory essays to various collections of printed source material.

Ritchie, R. L. G. THE NORMANS IN SCOTLAND. *Edinburgh University Press* 1954.
Describes the coming of the Normans and examines their impact on Scottish society.

Barrow, G. W. S. ROBERT THE BRUCE. *Eyre & Spottiswoode* 1965, 50*s*.
The best modern biography, written from a wide viewpoint and incorporating the results of modern research.

Barron, E. THE SCOTTISH WAR OF INDEPENDENCE. *Inverness, Carruthers* 1934, 12*s*. 6*d*.
Supplements Barrow on some points of detail.

Nicholson, R. EDWARD III AND THE SCOTS: the formative years of a military career, 1327–1335. *Oxford University Press* 1965, 30*s*.

Balfour-Melville, E. W. M. JAMES I, KING OF SCOTS. *Methuen* 1936.

Dunlop, A. I. THE LIFE AND TIMES OF JAMES KENNEDY, BISHOP OF ST. ANDREWS. *Edinburgh, Oliver & Boyd* (*St. Andrews University Publications*) 1950, 25*s*.
An extensive treatment, not limited to ecclesiastical affairs.

Mackie, R. L. KING JAMES IV OF SCOTLAND. *Edinburgh, Oliver & Boyd* 1958, 30*s*.

Paton, G. C. H., *ed.* AN INTRODUCTION TO SCOTTISH LEGAL HISTORY. *Edinburgh, Stair Society* 1958.

Relevant sections provide a basic guide to Scottish administration.

Barrow, G. W. S. THE ACTS OF MALCOLM IV. *Edinburgh University Press* 1960, 63*s*.

Introduction gives a detailed account of the Scottish central government during this reign: the first volume of a series of *Regesta Regum Scottorum* which will clarify the picture of Scottish government to the reign of James I.

Rait, R. S. THE PARLIAMENTS OF SCOTLAND. *Glasgow, Jackson* 1924, 30*s*.

Dickinson, W. Croft. SHERIFF COURT BOOK OF FIFE. *Edinburgh, Scottish History Society* (*3rd Series, Vol. 12*) 1928.

Important introduction.

Dickinson, W. Croft. COURT BOOK OF THE BARONY OF CARNWATH. *Edinburgh, Scottish History Society* (*3rd Series, Vol. 29*) 1957.

Important introduction.

Mackenzie, W. M. THE SCOTTISH BURGHS. *Edinburgh, Oliver & Boyd* 1949, 18*s*.

Dickinson, W. Croft. EARLY RECORDS OF THE BURGH OF ABERDEEN. *Edinburgh, Scottish History Society* (*3rd Series, Vol. 49*) 1957.

Important introduction.

Pryde, G. S. COURT BOOK OF THE BURGH OF KIRKINTILLOCH. *Edinburgh, Scottish History Society* (*3rd Series, Vol. 53*) 1963.

Important introduction.

(b) THE CHURCH

MacEwen, A. R. A HISTORY OF THE CHURCH OF SCOTLAND. 2 vols. *Hodder & Stoughton* 1913–18.

A history of the pre-Reformation Church.

Dowden, John. THE MEDIEVAL CHURCH IN SCOTLAND. *Glasgow, Maclehose* 1910.

Examines Church organisation in the mediaeval period.

Duke, J. A. HISTORY OF THE CHURCH OF SCOTLAND TO THE REFORMATION. *Edinburgh, Oliver & Boyd* 1937.

Simpson, W. Douglas. SAINT NINIAN AND THE ORIGINS OF THE CHRISTIAN CHURCH IN SCOTLAND. *Edinburgh, Oliver & Boyd* 1940.

Controversial.

Simpson, W. Douglas. THE CELTIC CHURCH IN SCOTLAND. *Edinburgh, Oliver & Boyd* (*Aberdeen University Studies*) 1935, 10*s*. 6*d*.

Duke, J. A. THE COLUMBAN CHURCH. *Edinburgh, Oliver & Boyd* 1957, 18*s*.

Simpson, W. Douglas. THE HISTORICAL SAINT COLUMBA. *Edinburgh, Oliver & Boyd* 1963.

Easson, D. MEDIEVAL RELIGIOUS HOUSES, SCOTLAND. *Longmans* 1957, 50*s*.
Lists basic information, but requires revision on some points of detail.

Coulton, G. C. SCOTTISH ABBEYS AND SOCIAL LIFE. *Cambridge University Press* 1933.

Easson, D. GAVIN DUNBAR. *Edinburgh, Oliver & Boyd* 1947, 10*s* 6*d*.
A brief biography of the Archbishop of Glasgow: describes the Church and ecclesiastical policies in the reign of James V.

(c) THE ECONOMY AND SOCIETY

Material for the study of the development of Scottish trade and society is sparse, but its examination has resulted in these interesting works.

Grant, I. F. SOCIAL AND ECONOMIC DEVELOPMENT OF SCOTLAND BEFORE 1603. *Edinburgh, Oliver & Boyd* 1930.

Franklin, T. B. A HISTORY OF SCOTTISH FARMING. *Edinburgh, Nelson* 1952.
Especially valuable for its study of the economic exploitation by the monks of the border abbeys of the natural resources of that region.

Davidson, J. and Gray, Sir Alexander. THE SCOTTISH STAPLE AT VEERE. *Longmans* 1909.
Scottish wool trade with the continent.

IV SIXTEENTH AND SEVENTEENTH CENTURIES

(a) POLITICS AND ADMINISTRATION

Mathieson, W. L. POLITICS AND RELIGION IN SCOTLAND, 1550–1690. 2 vols. *Glasgow, Maclehose* 1902.
Basic work for the political background.

Mathieson, W. L. SCOTLAND AND THE UNION, 1695–1747. *Glasgow, Maclehose* 1905.

Continues the above work into the modern period.

Mackinnon, J. THE UNION OF ENGLAND AND SCOTLAND. *Longmans* 1896.

Pryde, G. S. THE TREATY OF UNION OF SCOTLAND AND ENGLAND. *Edinburgh, Nelson* 1950.

Analyses the text of the treaty.

Terry, C. S. THE SCOTTISH PARLIAMENT, 1603–1707. *Glasgow, Maclehose* 1905.

Rae, T. I. THE ADMINISTRATION OF THE SCOTTISH FRONTIER, 1513–1603. *Edinburgh University Press* 1966, 50*s*.

The older of these works on Scottish political history, valuable although they are, are now outmoded in some respects due to the discovery of new material and subsequent reinterpretation of old material, and a new political interpretation of this period and the following modern era is awaited. Biographical studies of political personalities provide much information for this period. Mary, Queen of Scots, was the most controversial figure in sixteenth-century Scotland, and biographies, many still strongly biased for or against the Queen, are so numerous as to require a special bibliography. The following should be noted:

Henderson, T. F. MARY, QUEEN OF SCOTS. 2 vols. *Hutchinson* 1905.

The standard biography: sound, detailed, and almost unbiased.

Macnalty, *Sir* Arthur. MARY, QUEEN OF SCOTS. *Johnson* 1960, 21*s*.

One of the more interesting of recent popular works.

Morrison, N. B. MARY, QUEEN OF SCOTS. *Studio* 1960, 25*s*.

Phillips, J. E. IMAGES OF A QUEEN. *Berkeley, University of California Press* 1965, 56*s*.

Discusses the growth of the dual legend of Mary, the innocent martyr or the adulterous murderess.

Gatherer, W. A., *ed.* THE TYRANNOUS REIGN OF MARY STUART. *Edinburgh University Press* 1958, 25*s*.

An edition of George Buchanan's writings on Mary: the editor attempts to demolish the Buchanan side of the legend.

Other important biographical studies are:

Brown, P. Hume. GEORGE BUCHANAN, HUMANIST AND REFORMER. *Edinburgh, D. Douglas* 1890.

Lee, Maurice du Pont. JAMES STUART, EARL OF MORAY. *New York, Columbia University Press* 1953.

Lee, Maurice du Pont. JOHN MAITLAND OF THIRLESTANE. *Princeton University Press* (*dist. Oxford University Press*) 1959, 48*s*.

Percy, *Lord* Eustace. JOHN KNOX. New edn. *J. Clarke* 1966, 17*s* 6*d*.

Willson, D. H. KING JAMES VI AND I. *Cape* 1956, cased 30*s*; 1963, paper 12*s* 6*d*.

Buchan, J. THE MARQUIS OF MONTROSE. *Oxford University Press* (*World Classics*) 1957.

Robertson, A. THE LIFE OF SIR ROBERT MORAY, 1608–1673. *Longmans* 1922.

Lang, A. SIR GEORGE MACKENZIE: his life and times. *Longmans* 1909.

Mackenzie, W. C. ANDREW FLETCHER OF SALTOUN. *Edinburgh, Porpoise Press* 1935.

(b) THE CHURCH

The history of the Church in the sixteenth century is dominated by the Reformation, and the emotions roused by this event still colour historical interpretations of it.

Fleming, D. Hay. THE REFORMATION IN SCOTLAND. *Hodder & Stoughton* 1910.
Gives a Protestant point of view.

McRoberts, D., *ed.* ESSAYS ON THE SCOTTISH REFORMATION, 1513–1625. *Glasgow, Burns* 1962, 70*s*.
Essays mainly written by Roman Catholic scholars; contains interesting new material.

Donaldson, G. THE SCOTTISH REFORMATION. *Cambridge University Press* 1960.
Thoroughly grounded on the original sources, and written from a more detached, but pro-Episcopal, viewpoint.

Shaw, D. THE GENERAL ASSEMBLIES OF THE CHURCH OF SCOTLAND, 1560–1600. *Edinburgh, St Andrews Press* 1964, 42*s*.

The inter-relation of Church and politics during this period was so extensive that the general histories give an adequate coverage of Church affairs. There is no single study of the Church itself for the seventeenth century, but the following detailed works, including some on religious ideas current at the time, should be noted:

Donaldson, G. THE MAKING OF THE SCOTTISH PRAYER BOOK OF 1637. *Edinburgh University Press* 1954, 30*s*.

Hewison, J. King. THE COVENANTERS. 2 vols. *Glasgow, Smith* 1913.
Detailed but biased account of the Covenanting movement; valuable appendices.

Foster, W. R. BISHOP AND PRESBYTERY. *S.P.C.K.* 1958.
The Scottish Church between 1661 and 1688.

Henderson, G. D. RELIGIOUS LIFE IN SEVENTEENTH-CENTURY SCOTLAND. *Cambridge University Press* 1937.

Anderson, D. THE BIBLE IN SEVENTEENTH-CENTURY SCOTTISH LIFE AND LITERATURE. *Allenson* 1936.

(c) THE ECONOMY AND SOCIETY

Lythe, S. G. E. THE ECONOMY OF SCOTLAND, 1550–1625. *Edinburgh, Oliver & Boyd* 1960, 30*s*.
Examines the growth of Scottish industry and commerce, and places it within its European setting.

Smout, T. C. SCOTTISH TRADE ON THE EVE OF UNION, 1660–1707. *Edinburgh, Oliver & Boyd* 1963, 50*s*.
Illuminates the economic background to the Union; deals mainly with commerce and the mercantile policies of merchants and the government.

Insh, G. P. SCOTTISH COLONIAL SCHEMES, 1620–1686. *Glasgow, Maclehose, Jackson & Co.* 1922.

Insh, G. P. THE COMPANY OF SCOTLAND TRADING TO AFRICA AND THE INDIES. *New York, Scribner* 1932.
An excellent account of the disastrous Darien expedition, based on a thorough examination of the sources.

Conditions of society and the life of ordinary people in Scotland can more readily be understood from the time of the Reformation than for earlier periods.

Brown, P. Hume. SCOTLAND IN THE TIME OF QUEEN MARY. *Methuen* 1904.

Mathew, D. SCOTLAND UNDER CHARLES I. *Eyre & Spottiswoode* 1955, 30*s*.
Unreliable in places, but the only book to cover the subject for this period.

Warrack, J. DOMESTIC LIFE IN SCOTLAND, 1488–1688. *Methuen* 1920.

Ferguson, T. THE DAWN OF SCOTTISH SOCIAL WELFARE. *Edinburgh, Nelson* 1948.
Discusses epidemic diseases and medical care, housing, and relief of destitution from late mediaeval times to the mid-nineteenth century.

V MODERN SCOTLAND

(a) POLITICS AND ADMINISTRATION

There are a number of general works continuing the political history of the country to 1843, but no comprehensive work for the period after that, where one must rely on specialised studies and biographies.

(1) *General Works*

Mathieson, W. L. THE AWAKENING OF SCOTLAND, 1747–1797. *Glasgow, Maclehose* 1910.

Mathieson, W. L. CHURCH AND REFORM IN SCOTLAND, 1797–1843. *Glasgow, Maclehose* 1916.

Craik, *Sir* Henry. A CENTURY OF SCOTTISH HISTORY. *Edinburgh, Blackwood* 1901.
Covers the period from the Union to the Disruption.

(2) *Special Topics*

Riley, P. W. J. THE ENGLISH MINISTERS IN SCOTLAND, 1707–1727. *Athlone Press* 1964, 42*s*.
The impact of English government on Scotland immediately after the Union.

Meikle, H. W. SCOTLAND AND THE FRENCH REVOLUTION. *Glasgow, Maclehose* 1912.
The effect of revolutionary movements on Scottish politics and society.

Wright, L. C. SCOTTISH CHARTISM. *Edinburgh, Oliver & Boyd* 1953, 21*s*.

Young, Douglas. EDINBURGH IN THE AGE OF SIR WALTER SCOTT. *Norman, University of Oklahoma Press* 1965, $2.75.

Middlemas, R. K. THE CLYDESIDERS. *Hutchinson* 1965, 50*s*.

Coupland, *Sir* Reginald. WELSH AND SCOTTISH NATIONALISM. *Collins* 1954.
Inadequate for Scotland, but the only historical work to touch on this important subject.

(3) *Biographies*

Menary, G. THE LIFE AND LETTERS OF DUNCAN FORBES OF CULLODEN, 1685–1747. *Glasgow, Maclehose* 1936.

Furber, H. HENRY DUNDAS, FIRST VISCOUNT MELVILLE. *Oxford University Press* 1931.

Matheson, C. THE LIFE OF HENRY DUNDAS, FIRST VISCOUNT MELVILLE. *Constable* 1933.
Less clear and precise than the above work.

Mackie, J. B. LIFE AND WORK OF DUNCAN MACLAREN. 2 vols. *Edinburgh, Nelson* 1888.

Crewe, *Marquis of.* LORD ROSEBERY. 2 vols. *John Murray* 1931.

James, R. R. ROSEBERY. *Weidenfeld & Nicolson* 1963, 50*s*.

(4) *The Highlands*

The history of the Highland region and its special problems has often been virtually ignored in general works on Scottish history. Only the story of the Jacobite movement, and of the Highland Clearances, have produced many works, and these are of varied quality. The following should be noted:

Kermack, W. R. THE SCOTTISH HIGHLANDS: a short history. *Edinburgh, Johnston & Bacon* 1957, 9*s* 6*d*.

Mackenzie, W. C. THE HIGHLANDS AND ISLES OF SCOTLAND: a historical survey. *Edinburgh, Moray Press* 1949.
More detailed than the above work.

Cunningham, A. THE LOYAL CLANS. *Cambridge University Press* 1932.
The attitudes of the Jacobite clans, discussed within the framework of the relationship between the Scottish government and the Highlands from mediaeval times.

Prebble, J. GLENCOE: the story of the massacre. *Secker & Warburg* 1966, 42*s*.

Terry, C. S. THE RISING OF 1745. *David Nutt* 1903.
With a valuable bibliography.

Petrie, *Sir* Charles A. THE JACOBITE MOVEMENT. *Eyre & Spottiswoode* 1959, 42*s*.

Insh, G. P. THE SCOTTISH JACOBITE MOVEMENT. *Edinburgh, Moray Press* 1952.

Fergusson of Kilkerran, *Sir* James. ARGYLL IN THE FORTY-FIVE. *Faber* 1951.

Prebble, J. CULLODEN. *Secker & Warburg* 1961, 42*s*. *Penguin* 1967, 8*s* 6*d*.

Mackenzie, A. HISTORY OF HIGHLAND CLEARANCES. 2nd edn. *Glasgow, Maclaren* 1946, 17*s* 6*d*.

Prebble, J. THE HIGHLAND CLEARANCES. *Secker & Warburg* 1963. 42*s*.

Grimble, I. THE TRIAL OF PATRICK SELLAR. *Routledge & Kegan Paul* 1962, 28*s*.

Gray, M. THE HIGHLAND ECONOMY, 1750–1850. *Edinburgh, Oliver & Boyd* 1957, 30*s*.

Collier, A. THE CROFTING PROBLEM. *Cambridge University Press* 1953, 25*s*.

Day, J. P. PUBLIC ADMINISTRATION IN THE HIGHLANDS AND ISLANDS OF SCOTLAND. *University of London Press* 1918.

JOHNSTON'S CLAN HISTORIES. *Edinburgh, Johnston & Bacon* 1952, 5*s* and 6*s* each.

A numerous series of very good small volumes on individual clans.

Grant, Isobel F. THE MACLEODS: the history of a clan, 1200–1956. *Faber* 1959, 42*s*.

Other clan histories of comparable extent are much older and long out of print.

Grant, Isobel F. HIGHLAND FOLK WAYS. *Routledge & Kegan Paul* 1961, 40*s*.

Murray, W. H. HIGHLAND LANDSCAPE. *Edinburgh, National Trust for Scotland* 1962, 15*s*.

O'Dell, A. C. and Walton, K. THE HIGHLANDS AND ISLANDS OF SCOTLAND. *Nelson* 1962, 63*s*.

(b) THE CHURCH

Scottish ecclesiastical history after the Union is marked by the numbers of different denominations, many of them offshoots of the mainstream of the Presbyterian Church, each of which has its own separate history. The Church in general is discussed in the volumes by W. L. Mathieson already mentioned.

Fleming, J. R. HISTORY OF THE CHURCH IN SCOTLAND, 1843–1929. 2 vols. *Edinburgh, Clark* 1927–33, 12*s* 6*d*., 16*s*.

Watt, Hugh. THOMAS CHALMERS AND THE DISRUPTION. *Edinburgh, Nelson* 1943.

Surveys ecclesiastical politics at a significant point.

Sjölinder, Rolf. PRESBYTERIAN REUNION IN SCOTLAND, 1907–1921. *Edinburgh, Clark* 1964, 25*s*. *Stockholm, Almqvist & Wiksell*, 1962.

Bellesheim, A. HISTORY OF THE CATHOLIC CHURCH IN SCOTLAND. *Edinburgh, Blackwood* 1889–90.

For more recent work on the Catholic Church, reference should be made to articles in the INNES REVIEW, published twice yearly by *Burns, Glasgow*.

Goldie, F. SHORT HISTORY OF THE EPISCOPAL CHURCH IN SCOTLAND. *S.P.C.K.* 1951, 8*s* 6*d*.

Escott, H. A HISTORY OF SCOTTISH CONGREGATIONALISM. *Glasgow, Congregational Union of Scotland* (*dist. Edinburgh, J. Grant*) 1960, 15*s*.

Yuille, G. HISTORY OF THE BAPTISTS IN SCOTLAND. *Glasgow, Baptist Union Publication Committee* 1927.

Burnet, G. B. THE STORY OF QUAKERISM IN SCOTLAND. *James Clarke* 1952.

Perry W. THE OXFORD MOVEMENT IN SCOTLAND. *Cambridge University Press* 1933.

(c) THE ECONOMY AND SOCIETY

(1) *Agriculture*

Symon, J. A. SCOTTISH FARMING, PAST AND PRESENT. *Edinburgh, Oliver & Boyd* 1959.

Handley, J. E. SCOTTISH FARMING IN THE EIGHTEENTH CENTURY. *Faber* 1953.

Handley, J. E. THE AGRICULTURAL REVOLUTION IN SCOTLAND. *Glasgow, Burns* 1963.

Keith, James. FIFTY YEARS OF FARMING. *Faber* 1954.

Mitchison, R. AGRICULTURAL SIR JOHN. *Bles* 1962.

Sir John Sinclair of Ulbster, 1754–1835.

(2) *Industry and Commerce*

Campbell, R. H. SCOTLAND SINCE 1707. *Oxford, Blackwell* 1965, 35*s*.

Hamilton, H. THE INDUSTRIAL REVOLUTION IN SCOTLAND. *Oxford University Press* 1932.

Hamilton, H. ECONOMIC HISTORY OF SCOTLAND IN THE EIGHTEENTH CENTURY. *Oxford, Clarendon Press* 1963, 50*s*.

Marwick, W. H. ECONOMIC DEVELOPMENTS IN VICTORIAN SCOTLAND. *Allen & Unwin* 1936.

Marwick, W. H. SCOTLAND IN MODERN TIMES. *Cass* 1964, 30*s*.

Campbell, R. H. CARRON COMPANY. *Edinburgh, Oliver & Boyd* 1961, 30*s*.

Detailed study of the origins and growth of Scotland's first iron manufactory.

McKechnie, J. and Macgregor, M. A SHORT HISTORY OF THE SCOTTISH COAL-MINING INDUSTRY. *Edinburgh, National Coal Board, Scottish Division* 1958.

Arnot, R. Page. HISTORY OF THE SCOTTISH MINERS. *Allen & Unwin* 1956, 30*s*.

Shields, J. CLYDE-BUILT: a history of shipbuilding on the River Clyde. *Glasgow, Maclellan* 1949.

Kerr, A. W. HISTORY OF BANKING IN SCOTLAND. 4th edn. *A. & C. Black* 1926.

The financial background to the agricultural and industrial exploitation of Scotland's natural resources.

Clement, A. G. and Robertson, R. H. S. SCOTLAND'S SCIENTIFIC HERITAGE. *Edinburgh, Oliver & Boyd* 1961, 18*s*.

Development of scientific research in Scotland and its industrial significance.

Clow, A. and Clow, N. L. THE CHEMICAL REVOLUTION. *Batchworth* 1952.

Contains extensive sections on Scotland.

Payne, P. L., *ed.* STUDIES IN SCOTTISH BUSINESS HISTORY. *Cass* 1967, £5 5*s*.

Butt, J. INDUSTRIAL ARCHAEOLOGY OF SCOTLAND. *Newton Abbott, David & Charles* 1967, 50*s*.

Contains a gazetteer of industrial sites.

(3) *Transport and Communications*

Salmond, J. B. WADE IN SCOTLAND. *Edinburgh, Moray Press* 1938.

Construction of military roads in the eighteenth century.

Haldane, A. R. B. DROVE ROADS OF SCOTLAND. New edn. *Edinburgh University Press* 1968, 42*s*.
Traditional routes used by Highland drovers.

Haldane, A. R. B. NEW WAYS THROUGH THE GLENS. *Nelson* 1962, 35*s*.
Road construction in the early nineteenth century.

Gardiner, L. STAGE-COACH TO JOHN O'GROATS. *Hollis & Carter* 1961, 63*s*.

Nock, O. S. SCOTTISH RAILWAYS. *Nelson* 1961.

Prebble, John. THE HIGH GIRDERS. *Secker & Warburg* 1966, 25*s*.
The story of the Tay Bridge disaster.

Duckworth, C. L. D. and Langmuir, G. E. WEST HIGHLAND STEAMERS. 3rd edn. *T. Stephenson* 1967, 42*s*.

Donaldson, Gordon. NORTHWARDS BY SEA. *Edinburgh, John Grant* 1966, 30*s*.
History of the North of Scotland, Orkney and Shetland Shipping Co. Ltd.

(4) *Social Conditions*

Graham, H. G. SOCIAL LIFE OF SCOTLAND IN THE EIGHTEENTH CENTURY. New edn. *A. & C. Black* 1937.
Latest edition; first published in 1899. The classic work.

Plant, M. THE DOMESTIC LIFE OF SCOTLAND IN THE EIGHTEENTH CENTURY. *Edinburgh University Press* 1952, 25*s*.

Lochhead, M. THE SCOTS HOUSEHOLD IN THE EIGHTEENTH CENTURY. *Edinburgh, W. & R. Chambers* 1948, 12*s* 6*d*.

Haldane, E. S. THE SCOTLAND OF OUR FATHERS. *Glasgow, Maclehose* 1933.

Johnston, T. HISTORY OF THE WORKING CLASSES IN SCOTLAND. *Glasgow, Forward Publishing Co.* 1920.

Ferguson, T. SCOTTISH SOCIAL WELFARE, 1864–1914. *Edinburgh, E. & S. Livingstone* 1958, 42*s*.

Mechie, S. THE CHURCH AND SCOTTISH SOCIAL DEVELOPMENT, 1780–1870. *Oxford University Press* 1960.

Macdonald, D. F. SCOTLAND'S SHIFTING POPULATION, 1770–1850. *Glasgow, Jackson* 1937.
Analyses the growth of the population and its regional redistribution.

Handley, J. E. THE IRISH IN SCOTLAND, 1798–1845. *Cork University Press* 1943.

Handley, J. E. THE IRISH IN MODERN SCOTLAND. *Cork University Press* 1947.

Saunders, L. J. SCOTTISH DEMOCRACY, 1815–1840: the social and intellectual background. *Edinburgh, Oliver & Boyd* 1950, 21*s*.

VI SCOTS ABROAD

The influence exercised by Scotsmen overseas forms a significant part of Scottish history, but one which has not been surveyed completely by modern historians. The majority of the books, particularly on mediaeval aspects of this subject, are no longer easily obtainable, but are listed here for comprehensiveness. The eighteenth century has been most adequately surveyed; the great emigrations of the nineteenth century have not yet been fully analysed in a historical work.

Burton, J. H. THE SCOT ABROAD. 2 vols. *Edinburgh, Blackwood* 1864.
The first volume examines the close link between Scotland and France in the middle ages.

Francisque-Michel. LES ECOSSAIS EN FRANCE. 2 vols. *Trübner* 1862.

Fischer, T. A. THE SCOTS IN GERMANY. *Edinburgh, Schulze* 1902.

Fischer, T. A. THE SCOTS IN EASTERN AND WESTERN PRUSSIA. *Edinburgh, Schulze* 1903.

Fischer, T. A. THE SCOTS IN SWEDEN. *Edinburgh, Schulze* 1907.

Berg, J. and Lagercrantz, B. THE SCOTS IN SWEDEN. *Stockholm, Norstedt & Soner* 1962.

Dow, J. RUTHVEN'S ARMY IN SWEDEN AND ESTHONIA. *Stockholm, Almqvist & Wiksell* 1965, 14 Kr.

Notestein, W. THE SCOT IN HISTORY. *Cape* 1947.

Gibb, A. Dewar. SCOTTISH EMPIRE. *Glasgow, Maclehose* 1937.
Scots in Canada, Africa, India, Australia, and New Zealand.

Donaldson, Gordon. THE SCOTS OVERSEAS. *Hale* 1966, 25*s*.

Dunn, C. W. HIGHLAND SETTLER. *Toronto University Press* 1953.
'A portrait of the Scottish Gael in Nova Scotia'.

Graham, I. C. C. COLONISTS FROM SCOTLAND: emigration to North America, 1707–1783. *Ithaca, N.Y., Cornell University Press* (*dist. Oxford University Press*) 1956, 36*s*.

Meyer, D. THE HIGHLAND SCOTS OF NORTH CAROLINA, 1732–1776. *Chapel Hill, N.C., University of North Carolina Press* 1961, $6.00.

Layburn, J. G. THE SCOTCH-IRISH. *Chapel Hill, N.C., University of North Carolina Press* 1962.

Emigration of Ulster Scots to North Carolina.

Shepperson, G. A. *ed.* DAVID LIVINGSTONE AND THE ROVUMA: a notebook. *Edinburgh University Press* 1965, 21*s*.

Macmillan, D. S. SCOTLAND AND AUSTRALIA, 1788–1850. *Oxford University Press* 1967, 75*s*.

VII GENEALOGY AND HERALDRY

Books on the genealogy of Scottish families abound, and it would be invidious to select particular items among them. The indispensible guides to this mass of genealogical literature are:

Stuart, Margaret and Paul, *Sir* J. Balfour. A GUIDE TO WORKS OF REFERENCE ON THE HISTORY AND GENEALOGY OF SCOTTISH FAMILIES. *Edinburgh, Oliver & Boyd* 1930.

Ferguson, Joan P. S. SCOTTISH FAMILY HISTORIES AND LIBRARIES IN WHICH THEY ARE TO BE FOUND. *Edinburgh, Scottish Central Library* 1960, 21*s*.

Heraldry has long played an important part in Scottish social life. The two classic works on Scottish heraldry, still immensely valuable to the serious student, are:

Mackenzie of Rosehaugh, *Sir* George. SCIENCE OF HERAULDRIE. *Edinburgh, Heirs of Andrew Anderson* 1680.

Nisbet, Alexander. A SYSTEM OF HERALDRY. 2 vols. Vol. I, *Edinburgh, J. MackEuen* 1722; Vol. II, *Edinburgh, R. Fleming* 1742.

The following more recent books provide material for the basic study of the subject:

Innes of Learney, *Sir* Thomas. SCOTS HERALDRY. 2nd edn. *Edinburgh, Oliver & Boyd* 1956, 50*s*.

An account of Scots Heraldry, with a bibliography, by the present Lord Lyon King of Arms.

Stevenson, J. H. HERALDRY IN SCOTLAND. 2 vols. *Glasgow, Maclehose* 1914.

Paul, *Sir* J. Balfour. HERALDRY IN RELATION TO SCOTTISH HISTORY AND ART. *Edinburgh, D. Douglas* 1900.

Adam, F. CLANS, SEPTS, AND REGIMENTS OF THE SCOTTISH HIGHLANDS. 7th edn. rev. by Sir Thomas Innes of Learney. *Edinburgh, Johnston & Bacon* 1965, 55*s*.
A compendium of historical, legal and ceremonial data, tartans, and information regarding Scottish clans and customs.

Moncreiffe, *Sir* Iain and Pottinger, Don. SIMPLE HERALDRY. 10th edn. *Edinburgh, Nelson* 1963, 21*s*.
A pictorial introduction to Heraldry and Genealogy.

VIII THE ARMED FORCES

THE ARMY

In books dealing with the history of all, or several, Scottish regiments, the information can only be of a general nature. The main detailed sources are the regimental histories, several having been published for every regular regiment at one time or another. A considerable number have also appeared concerning the history of auxiliary forces, such as Yeomanry, Volunteers, Fencibles and Militia.

There are numerous unit histories of all kinds, many now out of print and only available in specialised libraries. Most of the more recent histories have the name of the regiment as the main title, or part of it, and quotation of the military title is usually all that is necessary to identify available books.

As Scottish regiments are part of the British Army, much important Scottish material can be found in books dealing with the Army as a whole. A standard, though unfinished, work on early regimental history is Richard Cannon, HISTORICAL RECORDS OF THE BRITISH ARMY, a volume for each regiment being published between 1836 and 1853, originally under the patronage of William IV. These are used as a source by the authors of later publications, and even very recent regimental histories use Cannon as a basis for the chapters on the earlier periods.

Cannon refers to the regiments by their pre-1881 numbers, e.g. 1st Foot (Royal Scots), 21st Foot (Royal Scots Fusiliers). Other regiments, which received their now familiar titles in 1881 after the amalgamation of two old numbered units, are dealt with by Cannon as separate formations, e.g. 71st and 74th Foot, later the Highland Light Infantry. If the reader wishes to identify all books on a particular regiment it is necessary to become familiar with these numbers; they are the only indication of the unit's identity in all the older histories and are still used by military historians and specialised writers.

In the field of military costume some of the most useful material is found in books not dealing exclusively with Scottish matters. Reliable Scottish sections are included in W. Y. Carman, BRITISH MILITARY UNIFORMS, *Hill*, 1957, and THE HISTORY OF THE UNIFORMS OF THE BRITISH ARMY, published by *P. Davies* in 1941, since reprinted by *Norman Publications* who also published Vol. III in 1961. J. Telfer Dunbar, HISTORY OF HIGHLAND DRESS, *Edinburgh, Oliver & Boyd*, 1962, £5 5*s.* has reliable chapters on Highland military dress and weapons.

The references to Scottish uniform in these three books are immensely more valuable than in any publication still in print claiming to deal specifically with the subject. At the moment there is no single comprehensive standard work on Scottish uniform, and the serious student must become familiar with the specimens in the Scottish United Services Museum, and refer to its library and large collection of contemporary pictorial records. Important material is published in the JOURNAL OF THE SOCIETY FOR ARMY HISTORICAL RESEARCH, which contains a substantial number of articles on Scottish subjects, giving information not otherwise available except by original research.

The Divisional histories deal adequately with the tactical activities of Scottish units in the two World Wars. Reference can also be made to official and other general War histories, as many Scottish units were not in Scottish divisions.

The following list gives titles useful to the general reader, and includes some standard works.

Terry, C. Sandford. THE ARMY OF THE COVENANT, 1643–1647. 2 vols. *Edinburgh, Scottish History Society* (*2nd Series. Vol.* 16–17) 1917.

Dalton, C. THE SCOTS ARMY, 1661–1688. *Eyre & Spottiswoode* 1909.
The standard work on the period.

Maxwell, Sir Herbert, *ed.* THE LOWLAND SCOTS REGIMENTS. *Glasgow, Maclehose* 1918.

Grierson, J. M. RECORDS OF THE SCOTTISH VOLUNTEER FORCE, 1859–1908. *Edinburgh, Blackwood* 1909.
The standard reference book on Volunteers.

Kirkwood, J. B. THE REGIMENTS OF SCOTLAND. *Edinburgh, W. & R. Chambers* 1949, 7*s* 6*d*.

Scobie, I. H. M. THE SCOTTISH REGIMENTS OF THE BRITISH ARMY. *Edinburgh, Oliver & Boyd* 1942.

Maclennan, J. SCOTS OF THE LINE. *Edinburgh, W. & R. Chambers* 1953.

Watson, F. THE STORY OF THE HIGHLAND REGIMENTS. *A. & C. Black* 1915.

Murray, A. K. HISTORY OF THE SCOTTISH REGIMENTS OF THE BRITISH ARMY. *Glasgow, Thomas Murray* 1862.

Cromb, J. THE HIGHLAND BRIGADE: its battles and heroes. *Simpkin Marshall* 1886.

Laffin, J. SCOTLAND THE BRAVE: the story of the Scottish soldier. *Cassell* 1963.

Barnes, R. M. and Allen, C. K. THE UNIFORMS AND HISTORY OF THE SCOTTISH REGIMENTS. *Seeley Service* 1956, 35*s*.

Smitherman, P. H. UNIFORMS OF THE SCOTTISH REGIMENTS. *Hugh Evelyn* 1963, 63*s*.

Bulloch, J. M. TERRITORIAL SOLDIERING IN THE NORTH-EAST OF SCOTLAND, 1759–1814. *Aberdeen, New Spalding Club* 1914.

Keltie, J. S. A HISTORY OF THE SCOTTISH HIGHLANDS, HIGHLAND CLANS AND HIGHLAND REGIMENTS. 2 vols. *Fullerton* 1875. Also 1887, 6 vols.

Tullibardine, *the Marchioness of.* A MILITARY HISTORY OF PERTHSHIRE, 1660–1902. *Glasgow, Maclehose* 1908.

Bewsher, F. W. HISTORY OF THE 51st HIGHLAND DIVISION, 1914–1918. *Edinburgh, Blackwood* 1921.

Ewing, J. THE HISTORY OF THE 9th (SCOTTISH) DIVISION, 1914–1919. *John Murray* 1921.

Stewart, J. and Buchan, J. THE 15th (SCOTTISH) DIVISION, 1914–1919. *Edinburgh, Blackwood* 1926.

Thompson, R. R. THE 52nd (LOWLAND) DIVISION, 1914–1918. *Glasgow, Maclehose, Jackson & Co.* 1923.

Martin, H. G. HISTORY OF THE 15th (LOWLAND) DIVISION, 1939–1945. *Edinburgh, Blackwood* 1948, 25*s*.

Blake, G. MOUNTAIN AND FLOOD: the history of the 52nd (Lowland) Division, 1939–1946. *Glasgow, Jackson* 1950.

Salmond, J. B. THE HISTORY OF THE 51st HIGHLAND DIVISION, 1939–1945. *Edinburgh, Blackwood* 1953, 15*s*.

Ross, A. OLD SCOTTISH REGIMENTAL COLOURS. *Edinburgh, Blackwood* 1885.

Ferguson, J. THE SCOTS BRIGADE IN HOLLAND. 3 vols. *Edinburgh, Scottish History Society* (*Vols.* 32, 35, 38) 1899–1901.

The only published work on the numerous Scottish formations in the service of the United Netherlands, 1572–1782.

Forbes-Leith, W. S. THE SCOTS GUARDS IN FRANCE. 2 vols. *Edinburgh, Paterson* 1882.

The Scots men-at-arms and Life Guards in the service of France, 1418–1830. The standard work on the subject in English.

Seton, *Sir* Bruce and Grant, J. THE PIPES OF WAR. *Glasgow, Maclehose, Jackson & Co.* 1920.

A record of the achievements of pipers of Scottish and overseas regiments during the War, 1914–18.

Malcolm, C. A. THE PIPER IN PEACE AND WAR. *John Murray* 1927.

THE NAVY

There has been no Scottish Navy since the Union and the only work on the subject before the Union is:

Grant, J. OLD SCOTS NAVY, 1689–1710. *Navy Records Society* 1914, 40*s*.

Information on Scotsmen serving in the Navy can be found in various biographies, and the general histories of the Royal Navy.

THE AIR FORCE

The Auxiliary Squadrons were the main Scottish connection with the Royal Air Force, and information about them is included in general Air Force histories, and the many books currently in print dealing with squadrons and their aircraft. Two wartime publications deal with the Edinburgh and Glasgow Squadrons:

SQUADRON 603, CITY OF EDINBURGH FIGHTER SQUADRON: a record of some of its achievements. *Edinburgh, Pillans & Wilson* 1943.

Nancarrow, F. G. GLASGOW'S FIGHTER SQUADRON. *Collins* 1942.

3 Tourism

An account of the earliest visitors to Scotland can be found in EARLY TRAVELLERS IN SCOTLAND, *Edinburgh, D. Douglas* 1891. Until almost the beginning of the seventeenth century they came on business. Edward I's errand need not be described, Froissart came as an 'on the spot' historian, Aeneas Sylvius, later Pope Pius II, on a diplomatic mission, Jacques de Lalain to fight a duel with a Douglas and Jean de Beagué as a soldier. Fynes Moryson (1598) is the first real tourist, John Taylor, the Water Poet (1618), the first who undertook to make the journey on foot and Richard Frank (1656) the first who came for the fishing. These were swallows and the summer came with the eighteenth century. The 'tourist', however, took a little longer to arrive. Though Daniel Defoe had used the word 'tour' in 1724 to describe what we would now call a business trip it was Thomas Pennant, James Boswell, Dr John Leyden, Rowland Hill and others who established the word in its modern sense, though it should be noted that Dr Johnson confined himself to the word 'journey'. The favoured part of Scotland was the Highlands and Islands, no doubt from a desire to view the haunts and habits of its 'savage' inhabitants as well as from a love of natural, wild beauty. Literary visitors who have left accounts were James Hogg the Ettrick Shepherd, the Wordsworths, Maria Edgeworth and Charles Dickens and by that time the visitors were of many of the nationalities of Europe. (A list may be found in Vol. II of Sir Arthur Mitchell and C. G. Cash's CONTRIBUTION TO THE BIBLIOGRAPHY OF SCOTTISH TOPOGRAPHY, *Edinburgh, The Scottish History Society* 1917, under the heading 'Tours' or, more fully, in Sir Arthur's list in the PROCEEDINGS OF THE SOCIETY OF ANTIQUARIES OF SCOTLAND, Vol. 35, 39 and 44, *Edinburgh, for the Society* 1901, 1905, 1910.)

The following list has little in common with the discursive accounts of earlier times. Its aim is to serve the mobility of the modern traveller with a well-ordered, informative text accompanied by good illustrations, though text has been the criterion of choice. It has in mind a traveller interested in the works of man as well as of nature, and in the past as well as the present.

BOOKS

Allan, J. R. NORTH-EAST LOWLANDS OF SCOTLAND. *Hale* (*County Book Series*) 1952.

Automobile Association. ILLUSTRATED ROAD BOOK OF SCOTLAND. 1963.

Bain, Robert. THE CLANS AND TARTANS OF SCOTLAND. 4th edn. enl. and re-ed. by M. O. MacDougall. *Collins* 1966, 12*s* 6*d*.

Blake, George. THE FIRTH OF CLYDE. *Collins* 1952.

Bolton, G. D. SCOTLAND'S WESTERN SEABOARD. *Edinburgh, Oliver & Boyd* 1953, 21*s*.

Brander, Michael. HO FOR THE BORDERS. *Bles* 1964, 7*s* 6*d*.

Brander, Michael. OVER THE LOWLANDS. *Bles* 1965, 25*s*.

Cluness, A. T. THE SHETLAND ISLES. *Hale* (*County Book Series*) 1951.

Elder, Madge. TELL THE TOWERS THEREOF: the ancient Border story. *Hale* 1956.

Finlay, Ian. THE HIGHLANDS. *Batsford* 1963, 25*s*.

Finlay, Ian. THE LOTHIANS. *Collins* 1960, 8*s* 6*d*.

Gordon, Seton. THE HIGHLANDS OF SCOTLAND. *Hale* (*County Books Series*) 1952, 21*s*.

Gordon, Seton. HIGHLAND DAYS. *Cassell* 1963, 30*s*.

Hammond, R. J. W., *ed*. THE COMPLETE SCOTLAND. 9th edn. *Ward, Lock* (*Red Guides*) 1966, 21*s*.

Also available in parts: EDINBURGH AND DISTRICT. 15th edn. 1963, 8*s* 6*d*.; THE HIGHLANDS OF SCOTLAND. 14th edn. 1964, 8*s* 6*d*.; WESTERN SCOTLAND. 16th edn. 1966, 9*s* 6*d*.

Hogg, Garry. THE FAR-FLUNG ISLES: Orkney and Shetland. *Hale* 1961.

House, Jack. DOWN THE CLYDE. *Edinburgh, W. & R. Chambers* 1960, 3*s* 6*d*.

House, Jack. THE HEART OF GLASGOW. *Hutchinson* 1965, 30*s*.

Innes of Learney, *Sir* Thomas. THE TARTANS OF THE CLANS AND FAMILIES OF SCOTLAND. 7th edn. *Edinburgh, Johnston & Bacon* 1964, 35*s*.

Johnston also issue a series of clan histories at 6*s* each.

Jack, Mary and Blair, J. L. CHAMBERS'S GUIDE TO SCOTLAND. Rev. edn. *Edinburgh, W. & R. Chambers* 1963, 12*s* 6*d*.

JOHNSTON'S GAZETTEER OF SCOTLAND. 2nd edn. rev. by B. B. Hartrop and R. Rodger. *Edinburgh, Johnston* 1958.

Kersting, A. F., *photographer*. PORTRAIT OF EDINBURGH; text by G. Scott-Moncrieff. *Batsford* 1961.

Lang, Theo. THE BORDER COUNTIES. *Hodder & Stoughton* (*The Queen's Scotland*) 1957, 18*s*.

Lang, Theo. EDINBURGH AND THE LOTHIANS. *Hodder & Stoughton* (*The Queen's Scotland*) 1952, 18*s*.

Lang, Theo. GLASGOW, CLYDE AND THE GALLOWAY. *Hodder & Stoughton* (*The Queen's Scotland*) 1953, 20*s*.

Lang, Theo. THE KINGDOM OF FIFE AND KINROSS-SHIRE. *Hodder & Stoughton* (*The Queen's Scotland*) 1951, 18*s*.

Lindsay, Maurice. THE LOWLANDS OF SCOTLAND: Glasgow and the North. *Hale* (*County Books Series*) 1953, 18*s*.

Lindsay, Maurice. THE LOWLANDS OF SCOTLAND: Edinburgh and the South. *Hale* (*County Books Series*) 1956, 18*s*.

Linklater, Eric. EDINBURGH. *Newnes* 1960.

MacGregor, A. A. SKYE AND THE INNER HEBRIDES. *Hale* (*County Books Series*) 1953.

McLaren, Moray. THE SHELL GUIDE TO SCOTLAND. *Ebury Press* 1965, 50*s*.

Maclean, Calum I. THE HIGHLANDS. *Batsford* 1959.

The author justly claimed 'I write as a Gaelic-speaking Highlander interpreting the traditional background, culture and ways of life. To that I bring the scientific, continental training of a student of folk-culture'. The best account of the Highlands ever written 'from the inside'.

McLean, Ruari. EDINBURGH: SCOTLAND'S CAPITAL. *Edinburgh, Oliver & Boyd* 1967, 84*s*.

McNeill, F. Marian. THE SILVER BOUGH: a study of the national and local festivals of Scotland. 4 vols. *Glasgow, Maclellan* 1957– , 21*s* each.

Three so far published. Vol. I: Scottish Folklore and Folk Belief. Vols. II and III: A Calendar of Scottish National Festivals, 2 vols. Vol. IV: Scottish Local Festivals, to be published.

Marwick, Hugh. ORKNEY. *Hale* (*County Books Series*) 1951.

Maxwell, *Sir* John Stirling. SHRINES AND HOMES OF SCOTLAND. *Edinburgh, W. & R. Chambers* 1958, 30*s*.

Muirhead, L. R. SCOTLAND. 5th edn. *Benn* (*Blue Guides*) 1967, 50*s*.

Murray, W. H. THE HEBRIDES. *Heinemann* 1966, 30*s*.

Nairne, Campbell. THE TROSSACHS AND THE ROB ROY COUNTRY. *Edinburgh, Oliver & Boyd* 1961, 21*s*.

National Trust. SEEING SCOTLAND. *Edinburgh, National Trust* 1965, 5*s*.

Oakley, C. A. 'THE SECOND CITY.' 2nd edn. *Blackie* 1967, 45*s*.

Piehler, H. A. SCOTLAND FOR EVERYMAN. *Dent* 1963, 15*s*.

Reid, J. M. GLASGOW. *Batsford* (*British Cities and Towns*) 1956.

Scott-Moncrieff, George. EDINBURGH. 3rd edn. *Edinburgh, Oliver & Boyd* 1965, 25*s*.

Scott-Moncrieff, George. THE SCOTTISH ISLANDS. 2nd edn. *Edinburgh, Oliver & Boyd* 1961, 21*s*.

Scott-Moncrieff, Lesley. SCOTLAND'S EASTERN COAST. *Edinburgh, Oliver & Boyd* 1963, 25*s*.

Swire, Otta F. THE HIGHLANDS AND THEIR LEGENDS. *Edinburgh, Oliver & Boyd* 1963, 30*s*.

Swire, Otta F. THE INNER HEBRIDES AND THEIR LEGENDS. *Collins* 1964, 25*s*.

Trent, Christopher. MOTORING ON SCOTTISH BYWAYS. *Foulis* 1964, 25*s*.

Williamson, Kenneth and Boyd, Morton. A MOSAIC OF ISLANDS. *Edinburgh, Oliver & Boyd* 1963, 21*s*.

Wyness, Fenton. CITY BY THE GREY NORTH SEA: Aberdeen. *Aberdeen, Alex. P. Reid* 1966, 45*s*.

MAPS

2½″ ORDNANCE SURVEY. 5*s* 6*d* paper flat; 6*s* 6*d* paper folded.
The North and East Coast and all the southern half of the country covered.

1″ ORDNANCE SURVEY. 5*s* 6*d* paper flat; 6*s* 6*d* paper folded;
8*s* 6*d* mounted and folded.

Also tourist maps: so far published; BEN NEVIS AND GLENCOE; LOCH LOMOND AND THE TROSSACHS; CAIRNGORMS. 7*s* 6*d*. paper flat; 10*s* 6*d* paper folded; 15*s* mounted and folded.

½″ JOHN BARTHOLOMEW & SON. Half-Inch of Great Britain. Continuously revised and up to date. 4*s* paper; 6*s* cloth mounted.

¼″ ORDNANCE SURVEY. 4*s* 6*d* paper flat; 5*s* 6*d* paper folded; 7*s* 6*d* mounted and folded.

4 Arts and Crafts

I GENERAL

Finlay, Ian. ART IN SCOTLAND. *Oxford University Press* 1948.

Finlay, Ian. SCOTTISH ART. *Longmans for the British Council* 1945, 2*s*.

Tonge, J. THE ARTS OF SCOTLAND. *Routledge & Kegan Paul* 1939.

II ARCHITECTURE

(a) Books of a general, introductory nature

Reiach, Alan and Hurd, Robert. BUILDING SCOTLAND: a cautionary guide. *Edinburgh, Saltire Society* 1940.

Scott-Moncrieff, George, *ed.* THE STONES OF SCOTLAND. *Batsford* 1938.

Scott-Moncrieff, George and Gauldie, Sinclair. LOOKING AT SCOTTISH BUILDINGS. *Edinburgh, Serif Books* 1947.

Finlay, Ian. THE STORY OF SCOTTISH ARCHITECTURE. *Edinburgh, Douglas & Foulis* 1951.
For schools.

Hannah, I. C. STORY OF SCOTLAND IN STONE. *Edinburgh, Oliver & Boyd* 1934.

Lindsay, Ian. THE SCOTTISH TRADITION IN BURGH ARCHITECTURE. *Edinburgh, Nelson for Saltire Society* 1948.

Dunbar, John G. THE HISTORIC ARCHITECTURE OF SCOTLAND. *Batsford* 1966, £5 5*s*.

(b) Reference Books

Billings, R. W. THE BARONIAL AND THE ECCLESIASTICAL ANTIQUITIES OF SCOTLAND. 4 vols. *Edinburgh, Blackwood* 1852.

ILLUSTRATED GUIDE TO ANCIENT MONUMENTS, No. VI: Scotland. *H.M.S.O.* 1959.

ILLUSTRATED REPORTS OF THE ROYAL COMMISSION ON ANCIENT MONUMENTS IN SCOTLAND. *H.M.S.O.*
All the published volumes.

MacGibbon, D. and Ross, T. THE CASTELLATED AND DOMESTIC ARCHITECTURE OF SCOTLAND FROM THE TWELFTH TO THE EIGHTEENTH CENTURY. 5 vols. *Edinburgh, D. Douglas* 1887–92.

MacGibbon, D. and Ross, T. THE ECCLESIASTICAL ARCHITECTURE OF SCOTLAND FROM THE EARLIEST TIMES TO THE SEVENTEENTH CENTURY. 3 vols. *Edinburgh, D. Douglas* 1896–97.

(c) Works on special fields or architects

Howarth, Thomas. CHARLES RENNIE MACKINTOSH AND THE MODERN MOVEMENT. *Routledge & Kegan Paul* 1952, 62*s*.

Simpson, W. Douglas. SCOTTISH CASTLES. *H.M.S.O.* 1959.

Hay, George. THE ARCHITECTURE OF SCOTTISH POST-REFORMATION CHURCHES, 1560–1843. *Oxford, Clarendon Press* 1957, 70*s*.

EDINBURGH, 1329 to 1929. *Edinburgh, Oliver & Boyd* 1929.
Sexcentenary of Bruce Charter.

Youngson, A. J. THE MAKING OF CLASSICAL EDINBURGH. *Edinburgh University Press* 1966, 63*s*.

Crossland, J. Brian. VICTORIAN EDINBURGH. *Letchworth, Wayfair Publications* 1966.

Cruden, Stuart. THE SCOTTISH CASTLE. Rev. edn. *Edinburgh, Nelson* (*Studies in History and Archaeology*) 1963, 45*s*.

Hill, Oliver. SCOTTISH CASTLES OF THE SIXTEENTH AND SEVENTEENTH CENTURIES. *Country Life* 1953.

Tranter, Nigel. THE FORTIFIED HOUSE IN SCOTLAND. 4 vols. *Edinburgh, Oliver & Boyd* 1962–66, 21*s*, 25*s*, 30*s*, 30*s*.

Lindsay, Ian G. CATHEDRALS OF SCOTLAND. *Edinburgh, W. & R. Chambers* 1926.

Lees-Milne, James. THE AGE OF ADAM. *Batsford* 1947.

Fleming, John. ROBERT ADAM AND HIS CIRCLE. *John Murray* 1962, 45*s*.

Coltart, J. S. SCOTTISH CHURCH ARCHITECTURE. *Sheldon Press for S.P.C.K.* 1936.

MacKenzie, W. M. THE MEDIAEVAL CASTLE IN SCOTLAND. *Methuen* 1927.

Bolton, A. T. THE ARCHITECTURE OF ROBERT AND JAMES ADAM, 1758–1794. 2 vols. *Country Life* 1925.

Hussey, C. THE WORK OF SIR ROBERT LORIMER, K.B.E. *Country Life* 1931.

III PAINTING

There is no up-to-date general history of Scottish painting. For the period before Raeburn the most reliable account is the two chapters on Allan Ramsay and on Painting in Scotland in the eighteenth century in E. K. Waterhouse's PAINTING IN BRITAIN, 1530 to 1790, *Penguin* 1953, £5 5*s*. Other works:

Caw, J. L. SCOTTISH PAINTING PAST AND PRESENT, 1620–1908. *Edinburgh, Jack* 1908.
More than half devoted to the period after 1860.

Cursiter, S. SCOTTISH ART. *Harrap* 1949.
A shorter account suitable for the general reader.

Apted, Michael R. THE PAINTED CEILINGS OF SCOTLAND, 1550–1650. *Edinburgh, H.M.S.O.* 1966, 50*s*.

Smart, A. THE LIFE AND ART OF ALLAN RAMSAY. *Routledge & Kegan Paul* 1952, 30*s*.
A very scholarly work.

Armstrong, W. and Stevenson, R. A. M. SIR HENRY RAEBURN. *Heinemann* 1901.

Caw, J. L. WILLIAM MCTAGGART, R.S.A. *Macmillan* 1917.

Cunningham, A. THE LIFE OF SIR DAVID WILKIE. 3 vols. *John Murray* 1843.

Dibdin, E. R. RAEBURN. *P. Allan* 1925.

Gower, R. S. SIR DAVID WILKIE. *Bell* 1902.

Greig, J. SIR HENRY RAEBURN, R.A. '*The Connoisseur*' 1911.

Honeyman, T. J. THREE SCOTTISH COLOURISTS: Cadell, Hunter, Peploe. *Nelson* 1950.

Eleven quarto picture books issued by the *National Gallery of Scotland* include FORTY SCOTTISH PAINTINGS, 1958, and SELECTED SCOTTISH DRAWINGS, 1960.

Informative illustrated catalogues of memorial exhibitions of modern painters are published by the *Scottish Arts Council*; among those already issued are JOAN EARDLEY, 1964, and JOHN MAXWELL, 1963, the latter issued in association with the *Scottish National Gallery of Modern Art.*

IV SCULPTURE

Richardson, James S. THE MEDIAEVAL STONE-CARVER IN SCOTLAND. *Edinburgh University Press* 1964, 42*s.*

Allen, J. Romilly. THE EARLY CHRISTIAN MONUMENTS OF SCOTLAND. *Edinburgh, Society of Antiquaries* 1903.

Drummond, J. SCULPTURED MONUMENTS OF IONA AND THE WEST HIGHLANDS. *Edinburgh, Society of Antiquaries* 1881.

Graham, Robert C. THE CARVED STONES OF ISLAY. *Glasgow, Maclehose* 1895.

Halliday, T. S. and Bruce, G. SCOTTISH SCULPTURE: a record of twenty years. *Dundee, Findlay* 1946, 25*s.*

V CRAFTS

Bushnell, G. H. SCOTTISH ENGRAVERS: a biographical dictionary. *Oxford University Press* 1949.

Burns, T. OLD SCOTTISH COMMUNION PLATE. *Edinburgh, R. & R. Clark* 1892.

Finlay, Ian. THE SCOTTISH TRADITION IN SILVER. *Edinburgh, Nelson for the Saltire Society* 1948.

Fleming, J. A. SCOTTISH AND JACOBITE GLASS. *Glasgow, Jackson* 1938.

Fleming, J. A. SCOTTISH POTTERY. *Glasgow, Maclehose* 1923.

Murphy, B. S. SCOTTISH WROUGHT IRONWORK. *Batsford* 1904.

Wood, L. I. SCOTTISH PEWTER, WARE AND PEWTERERS. *J. A. Morton* 1904.

Finlay, Ian. SCOTTISH CRAFTS. *Harrap* 1948.

Allen, J. Romilly. CELTIC ART IN PAGAN AND CHRISTIAN TIMES. *Methuen* 1904.

Includes numerous Scottish examples.

Anderson, Joseph. SCOTLAND IN PAGAN TIMES. Rhind Lectures, 1st and 2nd Series. *Edinburgh, D. Douglas* 1886, 1883.

Anderson, Joseph. SCOTLAND IN EARLY CHRISTIAN TIMES. Rhind Lectures, 1st and 2nd Series. *Edinburgh, D. Douglas* 1881.

Warrack, John. DOMESTIC LIFE IN SCOTLAND, 1488–1688. Rhind Lectures. *Methuen* 1920.

Useful coverage of furniture, woodwork, textiles and other craft media.

Jackson, *Sir* Charles J. ENGLISH GOLDSMITHS AND THEIR MARKS. *Dover Publications (dist. Constable)* 1965, £6 10*s*.

Section on Scottish hallmarks is still the standard reference work, although much additional information now available.

Finlay, Ian. SCOTTISH GOLD AND SILVER WORK. *Chatto & Windus* 1956.

Cochran-Patrick, R. W. THE RECORDS OF THE COINAGE OF SCOTLAND. 2 vols. *Edinburgh, Edmonston & Douglas* 1876.

Drummond, James. ANCIENT SCOTTISH WEAPONS. *Edinburgh, Waterston* 1881.

Drawings by the author, introduction and notes by Joseph Anderson.

Jackson, J. I. W. and Whitelaw, Charles E. EUROPEAN HAND-FIREARMS OF THE SIXTEENTH, SEVENTEENTH AND EIGHTEENTH CENTURIES. *Warner* 1923.

Section by Whitelaw on Scottish pistols remains the standard reference work.

Swain, M. H. THE FLOWERERS. *Edinburgh, W. & R. Chambers* 1955.

Ayrshire white needlework and the women who worked it.

Harrison, E. H., *ed.* SCOTTISH WOOLLENS. *Edinburgh, National Association of Scottish Woollen Manufacturers* 1956.

Essays on technique and care of wools, checks and tartans.

Dunbar, J. Telfer. THE HISTORY OF HIGHLAND DRESS. *Edinburgh, Oliver & Boyd* 1962, £5 5*s*.

McLintock, H. F. OLD IRISH AND HIGHLAND DRESS. *Dundalk, Dundalgan Press* 1950, 25*s*.

Blair, Matthew. THE PAISLEY SHAWL. *Paisley, Gardner* 1904.

VI MUSIC

(a) *General*

Apart from the rich folk-music tradition, music in Scotland has shown little of the originality and vitality of either literature or painting, and its bibliography is not extensive. The only comprehensive history of Scottish music is that by Dr Henry G. Farmer, and it barely touches the 20th century. Information about later developments and composers must be sought in music dictionaries and encyclopaedias, or in periodicals. There are several works dealing with particular types of music in Scotland, and some of the collections of songs have useful historical notes and introductions. The most important of these are listed below.

Farmer, Henry G. A HISTORY OF MUSIC IN SCOTLAND. *Hinrichsen* 1947.

Dalyell, *Sir* John Graham. MUSICAL MEMOIRS OF SCOTLAND: with historical annotations and numerous illustrative plates. *Edinburgh, T. G. Stevenson* 1849.

Dauney, William. ANCIENT SCOTTISH MELODIES FROM A MANUSCRIPT OF THE REIGN OF KING JAMES VI: with an introductory enquiry illustrative of the history of the music of Scotland. *Edinburgh Printing and Publishing Co.* 1838.

Glen, John. EARLY SCOTTISH MELODIES: including examples from MSS. and early printed works, along with a number of comparative tunes. *Edinburgh, J. & R. Glen* 1900.

Collinson, Francis. THE TRADITIONAL AND NATIONAL MUSIC OF SCOTLAND. *Routledge & Kegan Paul* 1966, 63*s*.

Grant, John. PIOBAIREACHD: its origin and construction. *Edinburgh, J. Grant* 1915.

Manson, W. L. THE HIGHLAND BAGPIPE: its history, literature and music, with some account of the traditions, superstitions, and anecdotes relating to the instrument and its tunes. *Paisley, A. Gardner* 1901.

Millar, Patrick. FOUR CENTURIES OF SCOTTISH PSALMODY. *Oxford University Press* 1949.

Harris, David F. SAINT CECILIA'S HALL IN THE NIDDRY WYND: a chapter in the history of the music of the past in Edinburgh. *Edinburgh, Oliphant Anderson & Ferrier* 1899.

Elliott, Kenneth. MUSIC OF SCOTLAND, 1500–1700. *Royal Musical Association* (*Musica Britannica, Vol. XV*) 1957.

An anthology of the art-music of the Church and Court.

Campbell, Alexander. ALBYN'S ANTHOLOGY: or a collection of the melodies and vocal poetry peculiar to Scotland and the Isles. 2 vols. *Edinburgh, Oliver & Boyd* 1816, 1818.

Graham, George Farquhar. THE SONGS OF SCOTLAND, adapted to their appropriate melodies and illustrated with historical, biographical and critical notes. *Edinburgh, Wood* 1837 and various editions.

Chambers, Robert. THE SONGS OF SCOTLAND PRIOR TO BURNS: with the tunes. *Edinburgh, W. & R. Chambers* 1862.

Christie, William. TRADITIONAL BALLAD AIRS: arranged . . . from copies procured in the counties of Aberdeen, Banff and Moray. 2 vols. *Edinburgh, D. Douglas* 1876, 1881.

Boulton, Harold and others. SONGS OF THE NORTH: gathered together from the Highlands and Lowlands of Scotland. 3 vols. *J. B. Cramer* 1885–1926, various editions.

Greig, John. SCOTS MINSTRELSIE: a national monument of Scottish song. 6 vols. *Edinburgh, T. C. & E. C. Jack* 1892–95.

Moffat, Alfred. THE MINSTRELSY OF SCOTLAND: with historical notes. *Augener* 1895.

Moffat, Alfred. THE MINSTRELSY OF THE SCOTTISH HIGHLANDS: a collection of Highland melodies, with Gaelic and English words. *Bayley & Ferguson* n.d.

Burns, Robert. THE SONGS OF ROBERT BURNS: now first printed with the melodies for which they were written . . . with bibliography, historical notes and glossary by James C. Dick. *Hatboro, Pennsylvania, Folklore Associates* (*dist. Herbert Jenkins*) 1962, £5 5*s*.

Reprint of 1903 edition.

Diack, J. Michael. THE SCOTTISH ORPHEUS. 3 vols. *Paterson's Publications* 1922–37.

Kennedy-Fraser, Marjory and McLeod, K., *comps*. SONGS OF THE HEBRIDES. 3 vols. *Boosey & Hawkes* 1917–22, 60*s* each.

Shaw, Margaret F. FOLKSONGS AND FOLKLORE OF SOUTH UIST. *Routledge & Kegan Paul* 1955, 50*s*.

Campbell, Archibald. THE KILBERRY BOOK OF CEOL MOR. 2nd edn. *Glasgow, Piobaireachd Society* (*dist. Glasgow, John Smith*) 1953, 45*s*.

Ross, Roderick S. BINNEAS IS BORERAIG. 3 vols. *Edinburgh, MacDonald* 1959–64.

A collection of pibrochs.

Glen, John. THE GLEN COLLECTION OF SCOTTISH DANCE MUSIC. 2 vols. *Edinburgh, J. Glen* 1891, 1895.

Robertson, James S., *comp.* THE ATHOLE COLLECTION OF THE DANCE MUSIC OF SCOTLAND. *Edinburgh, Oliver & Boyd* 1961, 60*s.* In 2 vols. 70*s.*

A reprint of 1884 edition.

Royal Scottish Country Dance Society. THE SCOTTISH COUNTRY DANCE BOOK. Books 1–22. *Glasgow* 1932–63.

Music and directions for dancing.

(b) *Scots Folksong*

Because of the constant intertwining of the Scots literary and 'folk' traditions, it is not easy to furnish a list of works purely popular in character. The eighteenth-century collections, such as Allan Ramsay's and David Herd's, are all, to a greater or lesser extent, the fruit of this folk-literary collaboration. Robert Burns's work of collection and re-creation for the SCOTS MUSICAL MUSEUM was followed by a not dissimilar fusion of art and tradition in Scott's MINSTRELSY OF THE SCOTTISH BORDER. The nineteenth century saw a gradual change of emphasis, with the collections of men like Motherwell, Kinloch and Jamieson, and the scrupulous ballad editorship of Prof. F. J. Child in the United States made possible a new era of revolutionary advances in folksong scholarship. The great work of the Buchan dominie Gavin Greig brought into focus, for the first time, the various strands of folk poetry, literature and musical tradition in our popular heritage.

Thomson, William. ORPHEUS CALEDONIUS. *Hatboro, Pennsylvania, Folklore Associates* (*dist. Herbert Jenkins*) 1962, 84*s.*

Provided tunes for the TEA-TABLE MISCELLANY. Facsimile reprint of 1733 edition.

Johnson, James. THE SCOTS MUSICAL MUSEUM. *Hatboro, Pennsylvania, Folklore Associates* (*dist. Herbert Jenkins*) 1962, £10 10*s.*

Burns contributed over two hundred items. First published in 1787–1803 in 6 volumes. Facsimile reprint of 1853 edition.

Thomson, George. A SELECT COLLECTION OF ORIGINAL SCOTTISH AIRS. 6 vols. *Preston & Son* 1793–1841, and various editions.

Ritson, Joseph. SCOTTISH SONGS. 2 vols. *J. Johnston & J. Egerton* 1794.

Jamieson, Robert. POPULAR BALLADS AND SONGS. 2 vols. *Edinburgh, Constable* 1806.

Hogg, James. THE JACOBITE RELICS OF SCOTLAND. 2 vols. *Edinburgh, Blackwood* 1819, 1821.

Chambers, Robert. THE POPULAR RHYMES OF SCOTLAND. *Edinburgh, William Hunter* 1826 and 1842.

Kinloch, George R. ANCIENT SCOTTISH BALLADS. *Longmans* 1827.

Motherwell, William. MINSTRELSY, ANCIENT AND MODERN. *Glasgow, J. Wylie* 1827.

Maidment, James. SCOTTISH BALLADS AND SONGS. *Edinburgh, T. G. Stevenson* 1859.

Ford, Robert. VAGABOND SONGS AND BALLADS OF SCOTLAND. 2 vols. *Paisley, A. Gardner* 1899, 1901; one-volume edition, *Paisley, A. Gardner* 1904.

Greig, Gavin. FOLK-SONG OF THE NORTH-EAST. *Hatboro, Pennsylvania, Folklore Associates* (*dist. Herbert Jenkins*) 1963, £6 6*s*.

Facsimile edition of reprints from the *Buchan Observer*, 1907–11.

Greig, Gavin and Keith, Alexander. LAST LEAVES OF TRADITIONAL BALLADS AND BALLAD AIRS. *Aberdeen, Buchan Club* 1925.

Ord, John. BOTHY SONGS AND BALLADS. *Paisley, A. Gardner* 1930.

MacColl, Ewan. SCOTLAND SINGS. *Workers' Music Association, Scottish Branch* 1953.

For Scots traditional ballads in other collections, see:

Child, Francis James, *ed.* ENGLISH AND SCOTTISH POPULAR BALLADS. 5 vols. *Oxford University Press* 1965, £17 the set; *Dover Publications* (*dist. Constable*) 1966, 5 vols. 22*s* each. See also 'Bronson' in the Appendix.

VII THEATRE

There exists no full-scale contemporary history of the Scottish theatre as a whole. The most important publications are:

Jackson, John. THE HISTORY OF THE SCOTTISH STAGE FROM ITS FIRST ESTABLISHMENT TO THE PRESENT TIME. *Edinburgh, for Peter Hill* 1793.

Jackson was for ten years manager of the Theatre Royal, Edinburgh.

Dibdin, James C. THE ANNALS OF THE EDINBURGH STAGE: with an account of the rise and progress of dramatic writing in Scotland. *Edinburgh, Richard Cameron* 1888.

Indispensable, if somewhat exasperating.

Lawson, Robb. THE STORY OF THE SCOTS STAGE. *Paisley, A. Gardner* 1917.

The following, many of which sketch the history of local enterprise, although some of them are little more than pamphlets, are worth consulting:

Topham, Edward. LETTERS FROM EDINBURGH WRITTEN . . . 1774 and 1775. *Dodsley* 1776.
Contains letters on the theatre.

MacKenzie, Donald. SCOTLAND'S FIRST NATIONAL THEATRE. *Edinburgh, Stanley Press* 1963.
The story of the original Theatre Royal, Edinburgh.

Mackie, A. D. and others. THE TWELVE SEASONS OF THE EDINBURGH GATEWAY COMPANY, 1953–1965. *Edinburgh, St Giles Press* 1965, 12*s* 6*d*.
Well illustrated. Contains a record of each season's performances.

Morris, James. RECOLLECTIONS OF THE AYR THEATRICALS. *Ayr Advertiser* 1872.

Boyd, Frank. RECORDS OF THE DUNDEE STAGE FROM THE EARLIEST TIMES TO THE PRESENT DAY. *Dundee, W. & D. C. Thomson* 1886.

Baynham, Walter. THE GLASGOW STAGE. *Glasgow, Robert Forrester*, 1892.

Glasgow Citizen's Theatre. A CONSPECTUS TO MARK THE CITIZEN'S 21st ANNIVERSARY AS A LIVING THEATRE IN GORBALS STREET, GLASGOW, 1943–1964, by various contributors. *Glasgow Citizen's Theatre* 1964, unpriced.

Bulloch, J. M. THE PLAYHOUSE OF BON-ACCORD. *Aberdeen, printed for the author* 1906.
Surveys briefly 'the actor's art in Aberdeen from forgotten times to the erection of Her Majesty's Theatre'.

Baxter, Peter. THE DRAMA IN PERTH. *Perth, Hunter* 1907.
Notices, early plays, playhouses, play-bills and pageants.

Gourlay, Jack and Saunders, R. C., *eds.* THE STORY OF GLASGOW CITIZEN'S THEATRE, 1943–48; introduced by James Bridie. *Stage & Screen Press* 1948.

Robertson, Alec. HISTORY OF DUNDEE THEATRE. *Precision Press* 1949.

Marford, Charles. THE BYRE STORMERS. *Anstruther* n.d.
Describes foundation and progress of the Byre Theatre, St. Andrews.

Bridie, James. DRAMATURGY IN SCOTLAND. *Glasgow, Royal Philosophical Society* 1949.
An address to the Royal Philosophical Society of Glasgow.

Anonymous. THE SCOTTISH NATIONAL THEATRE VENTURE: its birth, history, work and influence, 1921–48. (The Scottish National Players.) *Glasgow* 1953.

Milne, Colin. THE THEATRE IN SCOTLAND. *Prestwick, Prestwick Press* 1949.

Several books have been written on the works of Sir James Barrie, and two on those of James Bridie, including:

Walbrook, H. M. J. M. BARRIE AND THE THEATRE. *White* 1922.

Hammerton, *Sir* John A. BARRIE: the story of a genius. *Sampson Low* 1929.

Asquith, Cynthia. PORTRAIT OF BARRIE. *Barrie & Rockliff* 1954.

Bannister, Winnifred. JAMES BRIDIE AND HIS THEATRE. *Barrie & Rockliff* 1955.

Luyben, Helen L. JAMES BRIDIE: clown and philosopher. *Pennsylvania University Press* (*dist. Oxford University Press*) 1965, 40*s*.

The principal playwrights are Sir David Lindsay (*c*. 1490–*c*. 1555), William Alexander, Earl of Stirling (1580–1640), Archibald Pitcairne (1652–1713), Allan Ramsay (1686–1758), John Home (1722–1808), Joanna Baillie (1762–1851), Robert Williams Buchanan (1841–1901), R. L. Stevenson (1850–94) and W. E. Henley (1849–1903), William Archer (1856–1924), Graham Moffat (1866–1951), Sir James M. Barrie (1860–1937), 'John Brandane' (Dr John MacIntyre, 1869–1947), Gordon Bottomley (1874–1948), 'James Bridie' (Osborne H. Mavor, 1888–1951), Eric Linklater, 'Gordon Daviot' (Elizabeth MacIntosh, died 1952), Robins Millar, Murray McClymont, Robert MacLellan, Joe Corrie, A. J. Cronin, T. Maclachlan Watson (died 1963), Aimée Stuart and L. Arthur Rose, 'Ian Hay' (John Hay Beith, 1876–1952), Robert Kemp (1908–1967), Alexander Reid, Sydney Goodsir Smith, William Douglas Home and Stewart Conn.

The following are modern editions of, or contain plays by some of the earlier of the afore-mentioned:

Lindsay, *Sir* David. ANE SATYRE OF THE THRIE ESTAITS, adapted by Matthew P. McDiarmid. New edn. *Heinemann Educational Books* 1967, 16*s*.

Alexander, William, *Earl of Stirling.* THE DRAMATIC WORKS. *Longmans* 1921.

Ramsay, Allan. THE WORKS OF ALLAN RAMSAY, *ed.* Burns Martin and Oliver. Vol. II. *Edinburgh, Scottish Text Society* 1953.
Contains 'The Gentle Shepherd'.

Home, John. DOUGLAS, ed. by Hubert J. Tunney. *Lawrence, University of Kansas* 1924.

VIII CINEMA

Ballantine, W. M., *ed.* SCOTLAND'S RECORD. *Edinburgh, Albyn Press* 1946.
See 'Moving Pictures' by Norman Wilson in this survey of modern Scotland.

Blake, T. A., *ed.* FIFTY YEARS OF SCOTTISH CINEMA, 1896–1946. *Glasgow, Scottish Educational Film Association with Scottish Film Council* 1946.

Hardy, Forsyth, *ed.* GRIERSON ON DOCUMENTARY. *Faber* 1966, 50*s*.

Oakley, C. A. FIFTY YEARS AT THE PICTURES. *Glasgow, Scottish Film Council* 1946.

Wilson, Norman. PRESENTING SCOTLAND: a film survey. *Edinburgh, Edinburgh Film Guild* 1945.

SCOTLAND ON THE SCREEN. *Edinburgh, Films of Scotland Committee* 1961.

THE EDUCATIONAL FILM IN SCOTLAND. *Glasgow, Scottish Educational Film Association* 1956.
A twenty-first anniversary publication of the Association.

21 YEARS OF THE SCOTTISH FILM COUNCIL. *Glasgow, Scottish Film Office* 1955.

IX BROADCASTING

Burnett, George. SCOTLAND ON THE AIR. *Edinburgh, Moray Press* 1938.

Dinwiddie, Melville. THE SCOT AND HIS RADIO. *B.B.C. Publications* 1948.

B.B.C. YEAR BOOK. *B.B.C. Publications.*

THE FIRST THIRTY, 1923–1953: a picture book of thirty years'

Scottish broadcasting. *B.B.C. Publications* 1953.
Some text as well as illustrations.

FIVE YEARS OF SCOTTISH TELEVISION. *Glasgow, Scottish Television Ltd.* 1963.

SCOTTISH TELEVISION: some facts and figures. *Glasgow, Scottish Television Ltd.* 1963.

VISUAL EDUCATION ON SCOTTISH TELEVISION. *Glasgow, Scottish Television Ltd.* 1963.

X PRINTING (AND PUBLISHING)

Dickson, R. and Edmond, J. P. ANNALS OF SCOTTISH PRINTING FROM 1507 TO THE BEGINNING OF THE SEVENTEENTH CENTURY. *Cambridge, Macmillan & Bowes* 1890.
The standard work.

Aldis, H. G. A LIST OF BOOKS PRINTED IN SCOTLAND BEFORE 1700: including those printed furth of the Realm for Scottish booksellers with brief notes on the printers and stationers. *Edinburgh Bibliographical Society* 1904.
A new and greatly extended edition in preparation.

Beattie, William. THE CHEPMAN AND MYLLAR PRINTS: nine tracts from the first Scottish Press, Edinburgh 1508 . . . A facsimile with a bibliographical note. *Edinburgh Bibliographical Society* 1950.
Much information on the history of Scottish printing is also obtainable in the other publications of this Society and of the *Glasgow Bibliographical Society.*

MacLehose, J. THE GLASGOW UNIVERSITY PRESS, 1631–1931: with some notes on Scottish printing in the last three hundred years. *Glasgow University Press* 1931.
Contains a full account of the *Foulis Press.* Privately printed. Includes a bibliography.

Gaskell, Philip. A BIBLIOGRAPHY OF THE FOULIS PRESS. *Hart-Davis* 1964, £10 10*s*.

Beattie, William. THE SCOTTISH TRADITION IN PRINTED BOOKS. *Nelson for the Saltire Society* 1949, 2*s* 6*d*.
With illustrations.

Edmond, J. P. THE ABERDEEN PRINTERS: Edward Raban to James Nicol, 1620–1736. *Aberdeen, Edmond & Spark* 1886.

Johnstone, J. F. K. and Robertson, A. W. BIBLIOGRAPHIA ABERDONENSIS, 1472–1640, 1641–1700. 2 vols. *Aberdeen, Third Spalding Club* 1929–30.

Watson, James. THE HISTORY OF THE ART OF PRINTING . . . with . . . a preface by the publisher to the printers in Scotland. *Edinburgh, James Watson* 1713; facsimile edition *Gregg Press* (*English Bibliographical Sources, Series* 3, *Printers' Manuals*) 1965, 70*s*.

Beattie, William, *ed.* THE TAILL OF RAUF COILYEAR PRINTED BY ROBERT LEKPREUIK AT ST ANDREWS IN 1572: a facsimile of the only known copy. *Edinburgh, National Library of Scotland* 1966, 25*s*.

Berry, W. Turner and Johnson, A. F. CATALOGUE OF SPECIMENS OF PRINTING TYPES BY ENGLISH AND SCOTTISH PRINTERS AND FOUNDERS, 1665–1830. *Oxford University Press* 1935.
Also a supplement in *Signature* No. 16, N.S., 1952.

Isaac, Frank. ENGLISH AND SCOTTISH PRINTING TYPES, collected and annotated by Frank Isaac. 2 vols. *Oxford University Press for the Bibliographical Society* 1930–32, 70*s* each. Facsimiles and illustrations II and III.
For Scotland the period covered is 1501–1558.

Duff, E. Gordon. A CENTURY OF THE ENGLISH BOOK TRADE: short notices of all printers, stationers, book-binders . . . 1457 to 1557. *Oxford University Press for the Bibliographical Society* 1949, 40*s*.
Includes Scotland.

McKerrow, R. B., *general ed.* A DICTIONARY OF PRINTERS AND BOOKSELLERS IN ENGLAND, SCOTLAND AND IRELAND . . . 1557–1640. *The Bibliographical Society* 1910.

Plomer, Henry R. A DICTIONARY OF THE BOOKSELLERS AND PRINTERS WHO WERE AT WORK IN ENGLAND, SCOTLAND AND IRELAND FROM 1641 to 1667. *The Bibliographical Society* 1907.

Plomer, Henry R. and others. A DICTIONARY OF THE BOOKSELLERS AND PRINTERS WHO WERE AT WORK IN ENGLAND, SCOTLAND AND IRELAND FROM 1668 to 1725. *The Bibliographical Society* 1922.

Plomer, Henry R.; Bushnell, G. H. and Dix, E. R. MacC. A DICTIONARY OF THE BOOKSELLERS AND PRINTERS WHO WERE AT WORK IN ENGLAND, SCOTLAND AND IRELAND FROM 1726 to 1775. *The Bibliographical Society* 1932.
The Scottish section is by Bushnell. Supplements to this dictionary

in the PAPERS OF THE BIBLIOGRAPHICAL SOCIETY OF THE UNIVERSITY OF VIRGINIA.

Constable, Thomas. ARCHIBALD CONSTABLE AND HIS LITERARY CORRESPONDENTS. 3 vols. *Edinburgh, Edmonston & Douglas* 1873.

BRIEF NOTES ON THE ORIGINS OF T. & A. CONSTABLE LTD. *Edinburgh, Constable* 1936.

Wilson, *Sir* Daniel. WILLIAM NELSON: a memoir. *Edinburgh, Nelson* 1889.

Blackwood, J. C. THE EARLY HOUSE OF BLACKWOOD. *Edinburgh, Blackwood* 1900.

Oliphant, *Mrs* M. and Porter, *Mrs* Gerald. ANNALS OF A PUBLISHING HOUSE: Blackwood and his sons, their magazine and friends. 3 vols. *Edinburgh, Blackwood* 1897–8.

Nicolson, Alexander, *ed.* MEMOIRS OF ADAM BLACK. 2nd edn. *Longmans* 1885.

Blackie, W. W. JOHN BLACKIE SENIOR, 1782–1874. *Glasgow, Blackie* 1933.

Blackie, W. W. WALTER GRAHAM BLACKIE, 1816–1906. *Glasgow, Blackie* 1936.

Blackie, Walter Graham. SKETCH OF THE ORIGIN AND PROGRESS OF THE FIRM BLACKIE AND SON . . . 1809–1874. *Glasgow, Blackie* 1897.

Chambers, William. MEMOIR OF ROBERT CHAMBERS: with autobiographic reminiscences of William Chambers. 13th edn. *Edinburgh, W. & R. Chambers* 1884.

Keir, David E. THE HOUSE OF COLLINS: the story. *Collins* 1952.

FOOTPRINTS ON THE SANDS OF TIME, 1863–1963: the story of the House of Livingstone. *Edinburgh, E. & S. Livingstone* 1963.

Macleod, R. D. THE SCOTTISH PUBLISHING HOUSES. *Glasgow, W. & R. Holmes* 1953.

With important appendix of Selected References, largely bibliographical.

ADAM AND CHARLES BLACK, 1807–1957: some chapters in the history of a publishing house. *A. & C. Black* 1957.

Tredrey, Frank D. THE HOUSE OF BLACKWOOD, 1804–1954. *Edinburgh, Blackwood* 1954, 25*s*.

XI NEWSPAPERS

Couper, W. J. THE EDINBURGH PERIODICAL PRESS . . . from the earliest times to 1800. 2 vols. *Stirling, Mackay* 1908.
Craig, M. E. THE SCOTTISH PERIODICAL PRESS, 1750–1789. *Edinburgh, Oliver & Boyd* 1931.

Cowan, R. M. W. THE NEWSPAPER IN SCOTLAND: a study of its first expansion, 1815–1860. *Glasgow, Outram* 1946.

Ferguson, D. THE SCOTTISH NEWSPAPER PRESS. *Edinburgh, Saltire Society* 1946, 1*s*.

Ferguson, J. P. S. SCOTTISH NEWSPAPERS HELD IN SCOTTISH LIBRARIES. *Edinburgh, Scottish Central Library* 1956.
Kept up to date at the Scottish Central Library.
The Scotsman. THE GLORIOUS PRIVILEGE: THE HISTORY OF 'THE SCOTSMAN'. *Nelson for 'The Scotsman'* 1967, 35*s*.

5 Language and Literature

I SCOTTISH LANGUAGE

The history of Scots from its beginnings in Old Northumbrian, the northern dialect of Anglo-Saxon, in the seventh century, has been traced in detail in the classic, though now somewhat outdated, work of Sir James Murray, THE DIALECT OF THE SOUTHERN COUNTIES OF SCOTLAND, *Philological Society* 1876.

The Middle Scots period, fourteenth to sixteenth centuries, is also dealt with and illustrated in G. Gregory Smith, SPECIMENS OF MIDDLE SCOTS, *Edinburgh, Blackwood* 1902.

Since the late seventeenth century Scots survives chiefly as a literary medium for poetry, and occasionally drama, and in a series of regional dialects described with a grammatical and phonetic analysis in W. Grant and J. M. Dixon, MANUAL OF MODERN SCOTS, *Cambridge University Press* 1920. There are various works on single dialects:

Wilson, *Sir* James. LOWLAND SCOTCH. *Oxford University Press* 1915.
Perthshire.

Wilson, *Sir* James. THE DIALECTS OF CENTRAL SCOTLAND. *Oxford University Press* 1923.
Fife and Lothian.

Wilson, *Sir* James. THE DIALECT OF ROBERT BURNS. *Oxford University Press* 1926.
Ayrshire.

Watson, G. THE ROXBURGHSHIRE WORD-BOOK. *Cambridge University Press* 1923.

Jakobsen, J. AN ETYMOLOGICAL DICTIONARY OF THE NORN LANGUAGE IN SHETLAND. *Nutt* 1928.

Robertson, T. A. and Graham, J. J. GRAMMAR AND USAGE OF THE SHETLAND DIALECT. *Lerwick, 'Shetland Times'* 1952.

Marwick, H. THE ORKNEY NORN. *Oxford University Press* 1929.

An attempt to extend the literary range of modern Scots by reviving obsolete words and forms and by new creations has gone on under the influence of the poet Hugh MacDiarmid for the past thirty years. The 'new' language, known as 'Lallans' (Burns's name for Lowland Scots) has been championed in a pamphlet by Douglas Young, PLASTIC SCOTS, *Glasgow, Maclellan* 1948.

Scots vocabulary up to the beginning of the nineteenth century is set down in J. Jamieson, AN ETYMOLOGICAL DICTIONARY OF THE SCOTTISH LANGUAGE, *Edinburgh, W. Creech* 1808, enlarged in 1825, final edition in 5 vols., *Paisley, Gardner* 1875–87, an excellent work for its time and still the only complete Scottish dictionary, but now out-of-date in many details.

Warrack, Alexander. CHAMBERS' SCOTS DICTIONARY. New edn. *Edinburgh, W. & R. Chambers* 1952, 25*s*.

With a useful introduction on the history of the language by W. Grant.

A full and definitive record of Scots is now being compiled in two monumental dictionaries:

Craigie, *Sir* W. A. and Aitken, A. J. A DICTIONARY OF THE OLDER SCOTTISH TONGUE FROM THE TWELFTH CENTURY TO THE END OF THE SEVENTEENTH. *Chicago University Press* and *Oxford University Press* 1931– . Already published in 3 vols. 21 parts, A-L, 50*s*. per part. (Also Part 22, M- Mary.)

Grant, W. and Murison, David D. THE SCOTTISH NATIONAL DICTIONARY . . . containing all the Scottish words known to be in use or to have been in use since c. 1700. *Edinburgh, Scottish National Dictionary Association* 1931– .

6 vols. of 10 projected, A-O, already appeared. Also Vol. VII, Parts 1 and 2. Piner–Profite. £40 for the 10 vols.

II SCOTTISH PLACE-NAMES

Publications in this field largely belong to the period when the study of place-names was still the domain of the untrained amateur. Some of the 'classics' mentioned are consequently not necessarily included because of their reliability but as milestones in the development of this particular branch of linguistic research. Some of the best publications in this field have appeared in journals and periodicals rather than in books. The journal *Scottish Studies* for instance, has carried a regular series of articles on Scottish place-names ever since its inception in 1957.

Alexander, William M. THE PLACE-NAMES OF ABERDEENSHIRE. *Aberdeen, Third Spalding Club* 1952.

A first-rate work.

Forbes, Alexander Robert. PLACE-NAMES OF SKYE AND ADJACENT ISLANDS. *Paisley, A. Gardner* 1923.

A well-nigh comprehensive collection of Skye place-names, but the suggested etymologies are not always acceptable.

Jakobsen, Jakob. THE PLACE-NAMES OF SHETLAND. *Nutt* 1936.

A translation from Danish; derivations mostly reliable but difficult to handle because dialect and not standard forms are given for the names concerned.

Johnson-Ferguson, *Sir* Edward. THE PLACE-NAMES OF DUMFRIES-SHIRE. *Dumfries, Courier Press* 1935.

A good account of the place-names of this county.

Johnston, James B. PLACE-NAMES OF SCOTLAND. 3rd edn. *John Murray* 1934.

A revised version of the two previous editions (1892 and 1903). The only 'dictionary' of Scottish place-names available. Unfortunately most unreliable.

MacBain, Alexander. PLACE-NAMES. HIGHLANDS AND ISLANDS OF SCOTLAND. *Stirling, Mackay* 1922.

A collection of some of the author's best papers, edited by W. J. Watson.

Macdonald, Angus. THE PLACE-NAMES OF WEST LOTHIAN. *Edinburgh, Oliver & Boyd* 1941.

Authoritative.

Mackenzie, W. C. SCOTTISH PLACE-NAMES. *Kegan Paul* 1931.

Arranges names according to categories of meaning. Frequently speculative and linguistically unsound.

Marwick, Hugh. ORKNEY FARM-NAMES. *Kirkwall, W. R. Mackintosh* 1952.

Authoritative work.

Maxwell, *Sir* Herbert. THE PLACE NAMES OF GALLOWAY. *Glasgow, Jackson, Wylie* 1930.

Particularly strong in the collection of early spellings for each name. Many etymologies are suspect.

Watson, William J. PLACE-NAMES OF ROSS AND CROMARTY. *Inverness, Northern Counties Printing & Publishing Co.* 1904, 30*s*.

A pioneer work but still useful and usually reliable.

Watson, William J. THE HISTORY OF THE CELTIC PLACE-NAMES OF SCOTLAND. *Edinburgh, Blackwood* 1926.

The basic text-book for Scottish place-names of Celtic origin.

III LITERATURE, GENERAL

Good modern general works on Scottish literature and its background are few, and much important material is found only in scattered prefaces, essays, periodicals and older works of reference now out of print. The four following books, however, give between them a fairly comprehensive view of the subject:

Wittig, Kurt H. THE SCOTTISH TRADITION IN LITERATURE. *Edinburgh, Oliver & Boyd* 1958, 35*s*.
The only full-scale survey of Scottish literature from the fourteenth century to the mid-twentieth century. Fully documented. Select bibliography.

Kinsley, James, *ed.* SCOTTISH POETRY: a critical survey. *Cassell* 1955.
Essays by various hands, covering in chronological order the whole range of Scottish poetry in English and Scots, with a chapter on the Renaissance writers in Latin and a note on Gaelic poetry. Valuable notes to each chapter, bibliographical and general.

Spiers, John. THE SCOTS LITERARY TRADITION. 2nd rev. edn. *Chatto & Windus* 1962.
Critical and sociological essays emphasizing significant characteristics of Scottish poetic tradition from James IV to Hugh MacDiarmid.

Craig, David. SCOTTISH LITERATURE AND THE SCOTTISH PEOPLE, 1680–1830. *Chatto & Windus* 1961, 35*s*.
A fully-documented inquiry into 'the essentials of Scottish culture in relation to the literature and its public'. Its significance wider than the period stated.

Two recommended briefer surveys, both with helpful reading lists, are:

Wood, H. Harvey. SCOTTISH LITERATURE. *Longmans for the British Council* 1952, 3*s* 6*d*.
Mainly dealing with literature up to 1900.

Smith, Sydney Goodsir. A SHORT INTRODUCTION TO SCOTTISH LITERATURE. *Edinburgh, Serif Books* 1951.
Main interest in the modern movement.

The above-mentioned books can be supplemented by:

Grierson, *Sir* Herbert, *ed.* EDINBURGH ESSAYS ON SCOTS LITERATURE. *Edinburgh, Oliver & Boyd* 1933.
Informative on individual authors and topics.

Muir, Edwin. SCOTT AND SCOTLAND: the predicament of the Scottish writer. *Routledge* 1936.
Valuable insights into relations between individual talents and Scottish cultural background.

Power, William. LITERATURE AND OATMEAL: what literature has meant to Scotland. *Routledge* 1935.
Valuable insights into relations between individual talents and Scottish cultural background.

Smith, G. Gregory. SCOTTISH LITERATURE: character and influence. *Macmillan* 1919.
Remains the classic study of the distinctive features of the Scots literary tradition.

Indispensable among older works are:

Millar, J. H. A LITERARY HISTORY OF SCOTLAND. *Unwin* 1903.

Henderson, T. F. SCOTTISH VERNACULAR LITERATURE. Rev. edn. *Nutt* 1910.

General Collections and Anthologies

Eyre-Todd, George, *ed.* ABBOTSFORD SERIES OF THE SCOTTISH POETS. 6 vols. *Glasgow, Hodge* 1892–96.
The individual titles are MEDIAEVAL SCOTTISH POETRY. 2 vols., SCOTTISH POETRY OF THE 16th CENTURY, SCOTTISH POETRY OF THE 17th CENTURY, and SCOTTISH POETRY OF THE 18th CENTURY. 2 vols. All still very useful.

Dixon, W. M. THE EDINBURGH BOOK OF SCOTTISH VERSE, 1300–1900. *Meiklejohn & Holden* 1910.

Buchan, John. THE NORTHERN MUSE. *Nelson* 1924.

Fergusson of Kilkerran, *Sir* James. THE GREEN GARDEN. *Edinburgh, Oliver & Boyd* 1946, 5*s*.

MacDiarmid, Hugh. THE GOLDEN TREASURY OF SCOTTISH POETRY. *Macmillan* 1946, 8*s* 6*d*.

Mackie, R. L., *comp.* A BOOK OF SCOTTISH VERSE. *Oxford University Press* (*World's Classics*) 1956, 8*s* 6*d*.

Oliver, J. W. and Smith, J. C. A SCOTS ANTHOLOGY: poems in Scots, 13th to 20th century. *Edinburgh, Oliver & Boyd* 1949, 25*s*.

MacQueen, John and Scott, Tom, *comps.* THE OXFORD BOOK OF SCOTTISH VERSE. *Oxford, Clarendon Press* 1966, 45*s*.

Metcalfe, W. M. SPECIMENS OF SCOTTISH LITERATURE, 1325–1825. *Glasgow, Blackie* 1913.
Prose and verse.

Mackenzie, Agnes Mure. A GARLAND OF SCOTTISH PROSE. *House of Grant* (*dist. McGraw-Hill*) 1956, 7*s* 6*d*.

The Scottish Text Society has issued to its subscribers definitive critical editions of most of the Scottish poets and prose writers from Barbour (1316–95) to Robert Fergusson (1750–74). These are available in major reference libraries.

Saltire Society, Gladstone's Land, 483 Lawnmarket, Edinburgh 1. Among its publications are five vols. in *Saltire Modern Poets Series,* 1*s* 6*d*. each, *viz.* selections from the poems of George Bruce, 1947, Maurice Lindsay, 1947, Alexander Scott, 1950, Sydney Goodsir Smith, 1947, and Douglas Young, 1950. The *Saltire Classics* are:

SONGS AND LYRICS OF SIR WALTER SCOTT, ed. by Sir Herbert Grierson. 1942.

THE GUDE AND GODLIE BALLATIS, ed. by Iain Ross. 1957, 5*s*.

SELECTED POEMS OF JAMES HOGG, ed. by J. W. Oliver. 1946, 5*s*.

POEMS, EPISTLES, FABLES, SATIRES, ELEGIES AND LYRICS BY ALLAN RAMSAY, printed by T. Ruddiman 1721–28, ed. by H. Harvey Wood. 1946, 5*s*.

SELECTIONS FROM SIR THOMAS URQUHART OF CROMARTY, ed. by John Purves. 1942.

SCOTS POEMS BY ROBERT FERGUSSON, ed. by Alexander Law. 1947, 5*s*.

THE HISTORIE OF THE LYFE OF JAMES MELVILL: a selection, ed. by J. G. Fyfe. 1948, 5*s*.

POEMS BY SIR DAVID LYNDSAY OF THE MOUNT, ed. by Maurice Lindsay. 1948, 5*s*.

SELECTIONS FROM THE POEMS OF WILLIAM DUNBAR, ed. by Hugh MacDiarmid. 1952, 5*s*.

SELECTIONS FROM THE POEMS OF ROBERT HENRYSON, ed. by David Murison. 1952, 5*s*.

THE POEMS OF ALEXANDER SCOTT, 1525–84, ed. by Alexander Scott (his namesake). 1952, 7*s* 6*d*.

GAVIN DOUGLAS: a selection from his poetry, ed. by Sydney Goodsir Smith. 1959, 7*s* 6*d*.

ALEXANDER MONTGOMERIE: a selection from his songs and poems, ed. by Helena M. Shire. 1960, 7*s* 6*d*.

THE BRUCE, by John Barbour. A selection, ed. with an introduction by Alexander Kinghorn. 1960, 8*s* 6*d*.

THE HISTORIE OF THE REFORMATIOUN OF RELIGIOUN WITHIN THE REALM OF SCOTLAND BY JOHN KNOX, ed. by Ralph S. Walker. 1957.

IV LITERATURE TO 1700

The publications of the *Scottish Text Society* provide the most extensive collection of texts. Many are now out of print but reprints are to appear. Other series: *Saltire Classics, Clarendon Mediaeval and Tudor Series, Nelson's Mediaeval Texts.* Much supplementary material in club and society publications, especially those of the *Scottish History Society.* The most extensive bibliographies are in the CAMBRIDGE BIBLIOGRAPHY OF ENGLISH LITERATURE, 5 vols. *Cambridge University Press* 1940, Vols. I, II, III, V, 70*s*. each, Vol. IV: Index, 30*s*. and in W. L. Renwick and H. Orton, THE BEGINNINGS OF ENGLISH LITERATURE, 2nd edn. *Cresset Press* 1952. In addition to works listed under Literature: General, relevant criticism and literary history are found in:

Lewis, C. S. ENGLISH LITERATURE IN THE SIXTEENTH CENTURY (EXCLUDING DRAMA). *Oxford, Clarendon Press* (*History of English Literature, Vol. III*) 1954, 42*s*.

McRoberts, D., *ed.* ESSAYS ON THE SCOTTISH REFORMATION. *Glasgow, J. S. Burns* 1962, 70*s*.

Smith, J. M. THE FRENCH BACKGROUND OF MIDDLE SCOTS LITERATURE. *Edinburgh, Oliver & Boyd* 1934.

Important individual essays are found in:

Tillyard, E. M. W. FIVE POEMS, 1470–1870. *Chatto & Windus* 1948.

Spearing, A. C. CRITICISM AND MEDIEVAL POETRY. *Edward Arnold* 1964, 21*s*., 12*s* 6*d*.

Purves, J. in THE WORKS OF WILLIAM FOWLER, ed. by H. W. Meikle, Vol. III. *Edinburgh, Scottish Text Society* 1939.

Individual Authors (*chronological order*)

Barbour, John. THE BRUCE, ed. by W. W. Skeat. 2 vols. *Edinburgh, Scottish Text Society* 1894.

Barbour, John. THE BRUCE, ed. by W. Mackay Mackenzie. *A. & C. Black* 1909.

Barbour, John. THE BRUCE: a selection, ed. by A. Kinghorn. *Edinburgh, Saltire Society* 1960, 8*s* 6*d*.

Barbour, John. THE BUIK OF ALEXANDER, ed. by R. L. Graeme Ritchie. *Edinburgh, Scottish Text Society* 1921–29.

James I, *King of Scotland.* THE KINGIS QUAIR, ed. by W. Mackay Mackenzie. *Faber* 1939.

Blind Harry. THE WALLACE, ed. by J. Moir. *Edinburgh, Scottish Text Society,* 1885–89.
A new edition by M. P. McDiarmid in preparation.

Henryson, Robert. POEMS, ed. by G. Gregory Smith. *Edinburgh, Scottish Text Society* 1906–09.

Henryson, Robert. SELECTED POEMS, ed. by D. Murison. *Edinburgh, Saltire Society* 1952, 5*s*.

Henryson, Robert. POEMS AND FABLES, ed. by H. Harvey Wood. 2nd edn. rev. *Edinburgh, Oliver & Boyd* 1965, 35*s*.

Henryson, Robert. POEMS, ed. by C. Elliott. *Oxford, Clarendon Press* 1963, 21*s*.

MacQueen, John. ROBERT HENRYSON: a study of the major narrative poems. *Oxford University Press* 1967, 30*s*.

Henryson, Robert. TESTAMENT OF CRESSEID, ed. by Denton Fox. *Nelson* 1968, 21*s*.

Dunbar, William. POEMS, ed. by J. Small. *Edinburgh, Scottish Text Society* 1884–93.

Dunbar, William. SELECTION, ed. by Hugh MacDiarmid. *Edinburgh, Saltire Society* 1952, 5*s*.

Dunbar, William. POEMS, ed. by W. Mackay Mackenzie. *Faber* 1932, 25*s*.

Dunbar, William. POEMS, ed. by J. Kinsley. *Oxford, Clarendon Press* 1958, 18*s*.

DUNBAR: a critical exposition of the poems, by Tom Scott. *Edinburgh, Oliver & Boyd* 1966, 50*s*.

Douglas, Gavin. THE POETICAL WORKS, ed. by J. Small. *Edinburgh, W. Paterson* 1874.

Douglas, Gavin. THE AENEID, ed. by D. F. C. Coldwell. *Edinburgh, Scottish Text Society* 1951–65.

Douglas, Gavin. SELECTIONS, ed. by S. Goodsir Smith. *Edinburgh, Saltire Society* 1959, 7*s* 6*d*.

Douglas, Gavin. SELECTIONS, ed. by D. F. C. Coldwell. *Oxford, Clarendon Press* 1964, 18*s*.

Lindsay, *Sir* David. WORKS, ed. by D. Hamer. *Edinburgh, Scottish Text Society* 1930–34.

Lindsay, *Sir* David. POEMS, selected and ed. by M. Lindsay. *Edinburgh, Saltire Society* 1948, 5*s*.

Lindsay, *Sir* David. A SATIRE OF THE THREE ESTATES, ed. by R. Kemp. *Edinburgh, New Alliance and Scots Review* 1948.

Lindsay, *Sir* David. ANE SATYRE OF THE THRIE ESTAITS, ed. by J. Kinsley. *Cassell* 1954.

Lindsay, *Sir* David. SQUYR MELDRUM, ed. by J. Kinsley. *Nelson* 1959, 10*s*.

Scott, Alexander. POEMS, ed. by J. Cranstoun. *Edinburgh, Scottish Text Society* 1895.

Montgomerie, Alexander. POEMS, ed. by J. Cranstoun. *Edinburgh, Scottish Text Society* 1886–87.
With supplementary volume, ed. by G. Stevenson, 1907.

Montgomerie, Alexander. THE CHERRIE AND THE SLAE, ed. by H. Harvey Wood. *Faber* 1937.

Montgomerie, Alexander. SONGS AND POEMS, ed. by Helena M. Shire. *Edinburgh, Saltire Society* 1960, 7*s* 6*d*.

Drummond, William. POETICAL WORKS, ed. by L. E. Kastner. *Edinburgh, Scottish Text Society* 1911–12.

Other Collections of Particular Importance

SCOTTISH ALLITERATIVE POEMS, ed. by F. J. Amours. *Edinburgh, Scottish Text Society* 1892–97.

THE BANNATYNE MANUSCRIPT, ed. by W. Tod Ritchie. *Edinburgh, Scottish Text Society* 1928–32.

V LITERATURE AFTER 1700

Only authors central to the native Scots tradition are here treated in detail, except for the influential critics grouped around the *Edinburgh Review*. Emigrants and Anglo-Scots, e.g. Robert Blair,

Mark Akenside, James Thomson, Tobias Smollett and William Falconer, insofar as they bear relation to the Scottish tradition are discussed in A. M. Oliver's chapter on 'The Scottish Augustans' in the already mentioned SCOTTISH POETRY: a critical survey, ed. by J. Kinsley.

Another group, the 'Literati' or 'North Britons' of eighteenth-century Edinburgh were philosophers, theologians, historians, economists, etc., rather than imaginative writers. They figure prominently in general and period studies of Scottish intellectual history and in individual biographies such as E. C. Mossner's THE LIFE OF DAVID HUME, *Nelson* 1955, which also throw much light on the social and literary life of the capital.

Valuable among general studies of the period are:

Graham, H. G. SCOTTISH MEN OF LETTERS IN THE 18TH CENTURY. *A. & C. Black* 1901.

Daiches, David. THE PARADOX OF SCOTTISH CULTURE. *Oxford University Press* 1964, 12*s* 6*d*.

Thompson, H. W. A SCOTTISH MAN OF FEELING: some account of Henry Mackenzie and of the Golden Age of Burns and Scott. *Oxford University Press* 1931.

Both a biography and a social-literary history.

Among the personal reminiscences of the social and literary *milieux* are:

Carlyle, Alexander. AUTOBIOGRAPHY, ed. by J. H. Burton. *Edinburgh, Foulis* 1910.

Cockburn, Henry. MEMORIALS OF HIS TIME, ed. by W. F. Gray. *Edinburgh, Grant* 1946.

Cockburn, Henry. JOURNAL, 2 vols. *Edinburgh, Edmonston & Douglas* 1874.

Cockburn, Henry. SOME LETTERS, ed. by H. A. Cockburn. *Edinburgh, Grant & Murray* 1932.

Mackenzie, Henry. ANECDOTES AND EGOTISMS, 1745–1831, ed. by H. W. Thompson. *Oxford University Press* 1927.

Ramsay, *Dean* E. B. REMINISCENCES OF SCOTTISH LIFE AND CHARACTER. *Lane* 1947.

The Popular Poetic Revival

The primary texts, such as James Watson's A CHOICE COLLECTION OF COMIC AND SERIOUS SCOTS POEMS (1706–11), and Allan Ramsay's

collections, THE EVER GREEN (1724) and THE TEA-TABLE MISCELLANY are now difficult to obtain in any editions. Extracts from David Herd's ANCIENT AND MODERN SCOTS SONGS (1769 and 1776) are given in Hans Hecht's SONGS FROM DAVID HERD'S MANUSCRIPTS, *Edinburgh, W. J. Hay* 1904.
Collections and critical works bearing on aspects of the popular poetry include:

Scott, *Sir* Walter. MINSTRELSY OF THE SCOTTISH BORDER, ed. by T. F. Henderson. 4 vols. *Edinburgh, Blackwood* 1902.
The best edition.

Barke, J. and Smith, S. Goodsir, *eds.* THE MERRY MUSES OF CALEDONIA. *W. H. Allen* 1965, 30*s.*

Other collections and works of minor poets and song-writers of the period are noted in the afore-mentioned SCOTTISH POETRY: a critical survey, ed. by J. Kinsley, chapters vi, vii, and viii.

'Ossian'

Thomson, Derick S. THE GAELIC SOURCES OF MACPHERSON'S 'OSSIAN'. *Edinburgh, Oliver & Boyd for Aberdeen University* (*Aberdeen University Studies, No. 130*) 1951.

Smart, John S. JAMES MACPHERSON: an episode in literature. *Nutt* 1905.

Flower, Robin. BYRON AND OSSIAN. *Nottingham University* 1928.
These two works last-mentioned deal with the widespread influence of Macpherson's 'Ossian'.

Allan Ramsay, 1685–1758

Martin, Burns. ALLAN RAMSAY. *Oxford University Press* 1931.
A full-length study.

Gibson, Andrew. NEW LIGHT ON ALLAN RAMSAY. *Edinburgh, W. Brown* 1927.
An essay on controversial points of biography, etc.

Robert Fergusson, 1750–74

Fergusson, Robert. THE SCOTS POEMS, ed. by Bruce Dickins. *Edinburgh, Porpoise Press* 1925.

Fergusson, Robert. THE SCOTS POEMS, ed. by J. Telfer. *Edinburgh, Scottish Features* 1948.
With biographical sketch and notes.

Fergusson, Robert. THE UNPUBLISHED POEMS, ed. by W. E. Gillis. *Edinburgh, M. Macdonald* 1955.

Smith, S. Goodsir, *ed.* ROBERT FERGUSSON, 1750–74: essays by various hands. *Nelson* 1952.
An essential handbook.

Robert Burns, 1759–96

From the vast literature that includes editions, selections, biographies, critical works and bibliographies, the following have been chosen:

Egerer, J. W. A BIBLIOGRAPHY OF ROBERT BURNS. *Edinburgh, Oliver & Boyd* 1964, £5 5*s*.

Daiches, David. ROBERT BURNS. *Longmans for the British Council* (*Writers and Their Work Series, No. 88*) 1957, 3*s* 6*d*.
With a good selective bibliography.

THE POETRY OF ROBERT BURNS, ed. by W. E. Henley and T. F. Henderson. 4 vols. *Edinburgh, Jack* (*Centenary Edition*) 1896–7.
Best working edition, though not wholly reliable textually.

THE SONGS OF ROBERT BURNS: with their melodies, ed. by J. C. Dick. *Frowde* 1903.

BURNS: poetry and prose; with essays by Mackenzie, Jeffrey, Carlyle and others, ed. with an introd. and notes by R. Dewar. *Oxford University Press* 1929.

POETICAL WORKS, ed. by W. Wallace. *Edinburgh, W. & R. Chambers* (*Bicentenary Edition*) 1958, 32*s* 6*d*., 25*s*., 20*s*.

POEMS AND SELECTED LETTERS, ed. by A. Hepburn; introd. by D. Daiches. *Collins* 1959.

POEMS OF ROBERT BURNS, selected and ed. by H. W. Meikle and W. Beattie. *Penguin* 1958.

POEMS OF ROBERT BURNS, selected and ed. by L. Brander. *Oxford University Press* (*World's Classics*) 1950.

LETTERS, ed. by J. de Lancey Ferguson. 2 vols. *Oxford, Clarendon Press* 1931, 63*s*.

SELECTED LETTERS, ed. by J. de Lancey Ferguson. *Oxford University Press* (*World's Classics*) 1953.

Lockhart, J. G. LIFE OF ROBERT BURNS. *Dent* (*Everyman's Library*) 1959.

Snyder, F. B. THE LIFE OF ROBERT BURNS. *New York, Macmillan* 1932.

Hecht, H. ROBERT BURNS: the man and his work. 2nd rev. edn. *Edinburgh, Hodge* 1950, 12*s* 6*d*.

Daiches, D. ROBERT BURNS. 2nd rev. edn. *Deutsch* 1966, 42*s*.
A critical study.

Crawford, T. BURNS: a study of the poems and songs. *Edinburgh, Oliver & Boyd* 1960.

Snyder, F. B. ROBERT BURNS: his personality, his reputation and his art. *Oxford University Press* 1936.

Ferguson, J. de Lancey. PRIDE AND PASSION: Robert Burns, 1759–96. *Oxford University Press* n.d.
Critico-biographical.

Carswell, C. THE LIFE OF ROBERT BURNS. *Chatto & Windus* 1951.
Critico-biographical.

Campbell, W. B. A BURNS COMPANION. *Aberdeen, James Blair* 1953.

Lindsay, Maurice. THE BURNS ENCYCLOPAEDIA. *Hutchinson* 1959.

Thornton, R. D. JAMES CURRIE: the entire stranger, and Robert Burns. *Edinburgh, Oliver & Boyd* 1963, 63*s*.

Sir Walter Scott, 1771–1832

A good selective list of the vast Scott literature is appended to Ian Jack's SIR WALTER SCOTT, published by *Longmans for the British Council* (*Writers and Their Work, No. 103*) 1958, 3*s* 6*d*. Articles and monographs are listed in J. C. Corson's A BIBLIOGRAPHY OF SIR WALTER SCOTT, 1797–1940, *Edinburgh, Oliver & Boyd* 1943. Among good editions of the Waverley Novels are the Border edn., ed. by A. Lang, 48 vols., 1892–94; the Edinburgh edn., 48 vols., 1901–03, and the Oxford edn., ed. by J. L. Robertson, 24 vols., 1914, etc. There are also numerous popular reprints. W. M. Parker's prefaces and in most cases glossaries to the *Dent* (*Everyman's Library*) editions of the following Scott novels are worthy of mention: THE ANTIQUARY (1955, 15*s*.), THE BRIDE OF LAMMERMOOR (1955, 10*s* 6*d*., 7*s* 6*d*.), GUY MANNERING (1957, 12*s* 6*d*., 7*s* 6*d*.), THE HEART OF MIDLOTHIAN (1956, 10*s* 6*d*.), IVANHOE (1960, 12*s* 6*d*.), KENILWORTH (1959, 12*s* 6*d*.), OLD MORTALITY (1958, 12*s* 6*d*.), QUENTIN DURWARD (1960, 10*s* 6*d*.), REDGAUNTLET (1963, 10*s* 6*d*.), ROB ROY (1962, 10*s* 6*d*., 7*s*.), THE TALISMAN (1957, 12*s*., 6*s*.). Editions of other works, biographies and critical essays and studies are listed below:

SHORT STORIES, ed. by Lord David Cecil. *Oxford University Press* (*World's Classics*) 1934, etc.

POETICAL WORKS, ed. by J. L. Robertson. *Oxford University Press* (*Complete Edition*) 1894 and later reprints, 18*s*.

POEMS AND PLAYS, ed. by A. Lang. 2 vols. *Dent* (*Everyman's Library*) 1911.

THE LETTERS, ed. by Sir Herbert Grierson and others. 12 vols. *Constable* 1932–37.

THE PRIVATE LETTER-BOOKS OF SIR WALTER SCOTT, ed. by W. Partington. *Hodder & Stoughton* 1930.

THE JOURNAL OF SIR WALTER SCOTT, ed. by J. G. Tait. *Edinburgh, Oliver & Boyd* 1950.

Lockhart, J. G. MEMOIRS OF THE LIFE OF SIR WALTER SCOTT. 7 vols. *Edinburgh, Cadell* 1837–38.

Still the best biography. Often reprinted in its abridged form as THE LIFE OF WALTER SCOTT, e.g. *Dent* (*Everyman's Library*), introd. by W. M. Parker 1957, 12*s* 6*d*.

Grierson, *Sir* Herbert. SIR WALTER SCOTT: a new life. *Constable* 1938.

Supplements and corrects Lockhart.

Pearson, H. WALTER SCOTT: his life and personality. *Methuen* 1954, 25*s*.

Buchan, John. SIR WALTER SCOTT. 8th edn. *Cassell* 1961, 21*s*.

A biographical study with much sound critical comment.

Grierson, *Sir* Herbert. SIR WALTER SCOTT: broadcast-lectures to the young. *Edinburgh, Oliver & Boyd* 1932.

Muir, Edwin. SCOTT AND SCOTLAND. *Routledge* 1936.

Renwick, W. L., *ed.* SIR WALTER SCOTT LECTURES, 1940–48. *Gurney & Jackson* 1950.

Davie, D. THE HEYDAY OF SIR WALTER SCOTT. *Routledge & Kegan Paul* 1961.

Primarily a study of Scott's vogue and influence on the Continent.

James Hogg, The 'Ettrick Shepherd', 1770–1835

THE WORKS, rev. and ed. by T. Thomson, 2 vols. *Nimmo* (*Centenary Edition*) 1874.

THE PRIVATE MEMOIRS AND CONFESSIONS OF A JUSTIFIED SINNER, with a critical introd. by André Gide. *Cresset Library* 1947.

Batho, E. C. THE ETTRICK SHEPHERD. *Cambridge University Press* 1927.

With a good bibliography.

Strout, A. L. THE LIFE AND LETTERS OF JAMES HOGG. *Lubbock, Texas Technological College* 1946.

Simpson, L. JAMES HOGG: a critical study. *Edinburgh, Oliver & Boyd* 1962.

John Galt, 1779–1839

THE WORKS, ed. by D. S. Meldrum and W. Roughead. 10 vols. *Edinburgh, John Grant* 1936.

An incomplete edition containing only seven of Galt's novels. The earlier edition, ed. by D. S. Meldrum and S. R. Crockett, 8 vols. 1895–96, is also incomplete, but less so.

ANNALS OF THE PARISH *and* THE AYRSHIRE LEGATEES. *Dent* (*Everyman's Library*) 1910.

ANNALS OF THE PARISH, preface by W. M. Parker. *Nelson* (*School Classics*) 1952, 5*s* 9*d*.

THE ENTAIL, OR THE LAIRDS OF GRIPPY. *Oxford University Press* (*World's Classics*) 1913, etc.

Gordon, R. K. JOHN GALT. *Toronto University Press* 1920.

Aberdein, J. W. JOHN GALT. *Oxford University Press* 1936.

A biographical and critical study.

Frykman, E. JOHN GALT'S SCOTTISH STORIES. *Uppsala, A.-B. Lundequistska Bokhandeln* (*dist. Bailey Bros.*) 1959, 40*s*.

Important critical essays appear in the *John Galt Lecture Series* published as parts of the *Papers of the Greenock Philosophical Society*, notably W. M. Brownie, JOHN GALT, SOCIAL HISTORIAN, 1951, and W. Croft Dickinson, JOHN GALT, THE PROVOST AND THE BURGH, 1954.

John Gibson Lockhart, 1794–1854 (*as novelist*)

There is no collected edition of Lockhart's fiction and only two of his five novels have been re-issued:

PETER'S LETTERS TO HIS KINSFOLK (by Peter Morris). *Nelson* 1952.

SOME PASSAGES IN THE LIFE OF MR ADAM BLAIR. *Edinburgh University Press* (*Scottish Reprints, No. 1*) 1963.

Macbeth, Gilbert. JOHN GIBSON LOCKHART: a critical study. *Urbana, Illinois University Press* 1935, $2.25.

Susan Edmonstone Ferrier, 1782–1854

THE WORKS, with introd. by Lady M. Sackville. 4 vols. *Nash & Grayson* (*Holyrood Edition*) 1929.
Comprises her three novels MARRIAGE, THE INHERITANCE and DESTINY, together with a memoir and correspondence, ed. by J. A. Doyle.

MARRIAGE. *Nelson* (*School Classics*) 1953, 6*s* 6*d*.

David Macbeth Moir (*'Delta'*), *1798–1851*

THE LIFE OF MANSIE WAUGH, TAILOR IN DALKEITH, WRITTEN BY HIMSELF, introd. and notes by T. F. Henderson. *Edinburgh, Foulis* 1911.

Critics, Reviews, etc.

Lockhart, J. G. LOCKHART'S LITERARY CRITICISM, introd. and bibliography by M. C. Hildyard. *Oxford, Blackwell* 1931.

Lochhead, M. JOHN GIBSON LOCKHART. *John Murray* 1954, 25*s*.
A biography.

Jeffrey, F. JEFFREY'S LITERARY CRITICISM, ed. with introd. by D. Nichol Smith. *Oxford University Press* 1910.

Greig, J. A. FRANCIS JEFFREY OF THE EDINBURGH REVIEW. *Edinburgh, Oliver & Boyd* 1948.

Clive, J. SCOTCH REVIEWERS: a study of the 'Edinburgh Review'. *Faber* 1957.

VI 1850 TO 1920

As before, the list is confined to Scots who contributed to or influenced the later development of the native tradition, hence, e.g. John Davidson and James Thomson ('B.V.') are in, but not Carlyle and Mrs Oliphant.

(a) *Poetry*

The anthology SCOTTISH VERSE, 1851–1951, ed. by Douglas Young,

Nelson 1952, covers this period together with the 'Scottish Renaissance' that followed World War I.

Stevenson, Robert Louis. COLLECTED POEMS, ed. by J. Adam Smith. *Hart-Davis* 1950, 18*s*.
The only full critical edition.

Thomson, James ('B.V.'). THE CITY OF DREADFUL NIGHT AND OTHER POEMS, ed. by E. Blunden. *Methuen* 1932.

Thomson, James ('B.V.'). POEMS AND SOME LETTERS, ed. with a biographical and critical introd. by A. Ridler. *Centaur Press* 1963, 63*s*.

Walker, I. B. JAMES THOMSON ('B.V.'): a critical study. *Cornell University Press* (*dist. Oxford University Press*) 1950, 20*s*.

Davidson, John. JOHN DAVIDSON. *Benn* (*Augustan Books of Modern Verse*) 1925.

Davidson, John. POEMS AND BALLADS, selected with an introd. by R. D. Macleod. *Unicorn Press* 1959.

Davidson, John. JOHN DAVIDSON: a selection of his poems, ed. by Maurice Lindsay, with an essay by Hugh MacDiarmid. *Hutchinson* 1961.

Macleod, R. D. JOHN DAVIDSON: a study in personality. *Glasgow, W. R. Holmes* 1957.

Townsend, J. B. JOHN DAVIDSON: poet of Armageddon. *Yale University Press* 1961, 63*s*.

Buchan, John. POEMS SCOTS AND ENGLISH. *Jack* 1917.

Murray, Charles. HAMEWITH AND OTHER POEMS. *Constable* 1962, 18*s*.

Murray, Charles. A SOUGH OF WAR. *Constable* 1917.

Murray, Charles. IN COUNTRY PLACES. *Constable* 1920.

Aytoun, William Edmonstone. STORIES AND VERSE, with an introd. by W. L. Renwick. *Edinburgh University Press* (*Scottish Reprints, No. 2*) 1964, 20*s*.

(b) *Fiction*

Robert Louis Stevenson, 1850–94

See G. B. Stern's select bibliography appended to her R. L. STEVENSON, *Longmans for the British Council* (*Writers and Their Work Series, No. 52*), paper 3*s* 6*d*.

Recommended COLLECTED WORKS are the Tusitala edn., 35 vols., 1923–24, and the Skerryvore edn., 30 vols., 1924–26.

LETTERS, ed. by S. Colvin. 4 vols. *Methuen* 1911.

R. L. S. STEVENSON'S LETTERS TO CHARLES BAXTER, ed. by J. de Lancey Ferguson and M. Waingrow. *Yale University Press* (*dist. Oxford University Press*) 1956, 42*s*.

HENRY JAMES AND ROBERT LOUIS STEVENSON: a record of friendship and criticism, ed. by J. Adam Smith. *Hart-Davis* 1948.

Useful compendia and selections:

R.L.S.: an omnibus, selected and ed. by G. B. Stern. *Cassell* 1950.

NOVELS AND STORIES, selected by V. S. Pritchett. *Pilot Press* 1945.

STRANGE CASE OF DR. JEKYLL AND MR. HYDE, AND OTHER STORIES. *Macdonald* (*Illustrated Classics*) 1950, 15*s*.

ESSAYS. *Macdonald* (*Illustrated Classics*) 1950.

THE WRONG BOX, introd. by B. Darwin. *Oxford University Press* (*World's Classics*) 1954, 7*s* 6*d*. (Joint author with Lloyd Osbourne).

STEVENSON: a selection and commentary, ed. by M. R. Ridley. *Oxford University Press* 1953.

THE STEVENSON COMPANION, comp. by John Hampden. *Phoenix House* 1950.

Biographical and critical studies:

Balfour, G. THE LIFE OF ROBERT LOUIS STEVENSON. 2 vols. *Methuen* 1901.

Steuart, J. A. R. L. STEVENSON: man and writer. 2 vols. *Low* 1924.

Furnas, J. C. VOYAGE TO WINDWARD. *Faber* 1952, 25*s*.
The best modern biography.

Elwin, M. THE STRANGE CASE OF R. L. STEVENSON. *Macdonald* 1950, 12*s* 6*d*.

Daiches, D. ROBERT LOUIS STEVENSON. *Glasgow, Maclellan* 1947.
The best critical study.

'Kailyard' and 'Anti-Kailyard'

'Kailyard' fiction has been critically described by George Blake in BARRIE AND THE KAILYARD SCHOOL, *Barker* 1951, in which J. M. Barrie's AULD LICHT IDYLLS, *Hodder & Stoughton* 1888, and A

WINDOW IN THRUMS, *Hodder & Stoughton* 1889, together with similar works by the Rev. John Watson ('Ian Maclaren'), George Macdonald, and S. R. Crockett, are unfavourably contrasted with a few outstanding 'anti-Kailyard' novels, notably those of George Douglas Brown and J. MacDougall Hay. For the massive output of George Macdonald and S. R. Crockett see the CAMBRIDGE BIBLIOGRAPHY OF ENGLISH LITERATURE. Crockett's THE STICKIT MINISTER went into its 10th edition in 1895; his THE LILAC SUNBONNET and THE RAIDERS were re-issued in a single volume by *Collins* (*Classics Series*) in 1954, 10*s*., 8*s*.

Brown, George Douglas. THE HOUSE WITH THE GREEN SHUTTERS, with introd. by W. Somerset Maugham. *Oxford University Press* (*World's Classics*) 1938.

Veitch, J. GEORGE DOUGLAS BROWN. *Jenkins* 1952.
A full-length study.

Hay, J. MacDougall. GILLESPIE, preface by R. Kemp. New edn. *Duckworth* (*Leviathan Series*) 1963, 35*s*.

Other Novelists

Sharp, William ('Fiona Macleod'). THE WRITINGS OF FIONA MACLEOD. 7 vols. *Heinemann* (*Uniform Edition*) 1909–10; 8 vols. *Heinemann* (*Pocket Edition*) 1927.

Munro, Neil. THE WORKS. 9 vols. *Edinburgh, Blackwood* (*Inveraray Edition*) 1935.
There are many reprints of individual novels, 7*s* 6*d*. each. Munro and Sharp attempt to express a Celtic vision.

Buchan, John. THE TALES AND ROMANCES OF JOHN BUCHAN. 17 vols. *Nelson* 1922.
There are many reprints of individual works. The contribution to the native tradition is relatively small and largely in the historico-romantic vein.

Turner, A. C. MR BUCHAN, WRITER: a life of the first Lord Tweedsmuir. *S.C.M.* 1949.

VII 1920 TO THE PRESENT

The only full-scale study is Duncan Glen's HUGH MACDIARMID AND THE SCOTTISH RENAISSANCE, *Edinburgh, W. & R. Chambers* 1964, 37*s* 6*d*., containing the fullest bibliographies to date of MacDiarmid and of the 'Renaissance' movement as a whole.

Useful general introductions:

Reid, J. M. MODERN SCOTTISH LITERATURE. *Edinburgh, Saltire Society* 1945, 1*s*.

Lindsay, Maurice. THE SCOTTISH RENAISSANCE. *Edinburgh, Serif Books* 1948.

Blake, George. ANNALS OF SCOTLAND, 1895–1955. *B.B.C. Publications* 1956.
An illustrated guide to a series of radio adaptations, with useful commentary.

Young, Douglas. PLASTIC SCOTS AND THE SCOTS TRADITION. *Glasgow, Maclellan* 1948.

Anthologies:

Lindsay, Maurice, *ed.* MODERN SCOTTISH POETRY. 2nd edn. *Faber* 1966, 21*s*.

McCaig, Norman, *ed.* HONOUR'D SHADE. *Edinburgh, W. & R. Chambers* 1959.
An anthology of new Scottish poetry to mark the bicentenary of the birth of Burns.

Linklater, E., *ed.* THE THISTLE AND THE PEN. *Nelson* 1950.
An anthology of poetry, prose and drama.

Urquhart, F., *ed.* SCOTTISH SHORT STORIES. 3rd rev. edn. *Faber* 1957, 15*s*.

(a) *Poetry*

Forerunners of the modern movement include Violet Jacob (THE SCOTTISH POEMS OF VIOLET JACOB, *Edinburgh, Saltire Classics*, 1944), Marion Angus (SELECTED POEMS, *Edinburgh, Serif Books* 1950), Sir Alexander Gray (FOUR AND FORTY, *Edinburgh University Press* 1954, 12*s* 6*d*.), and Lewis Spence (COLLECTED POEMS, *Edinburgh, Serif Books* 1953).

Poets writing mainly in Scots:

MacDiarmid, Hugh. COLLECTED POEMS OF HUGH MACDIARMID. 2nd edn. *New York, Macmillan*; *London, Collier-Macmillan* 1967, $7.95.
Does not contain all his poems.

MacDiarmid, Hugh. A LAP OF HONOUR. *MacGibbon & Kee* 1967, 25*s*.
For bibliographies see Duncan Glen, already mentioned above,

and W. R. Aitken's checklist in *The Bibliotheck* Vol. I, No. 4, 1958.

Soutar, William. COLLECTED POEMS. *Dakers* 1948.

Soutar, William. DIARIES OF A DYING MAN. *Edinburgh, W. & R. Chambers* 1954.

Soutar, William. POEMS IN SCOTS AND ENGLISH, ed. by W. R. Aitken. *Edinburgh, Oliver & Boyd* 1961.

Scott, Alexander. STILL LIFE: William Soutar, 1898–1943. 3rd rev. edn. *Edinburgh, W. & R. Chambers* 1958, 25*s*.

Other contemporary poets who have published volumes of poems mainly in Scots include Sydney Goodsir Smith, George Campbell Hay, R. G. Sutherland ('Robert Garioch'), Douglas Young, R. Crombie Saunders, Maurice Lindsay, Alexander Scott, Tom Scott, Helen B. Cruikshank and J. K. Annand.

Poets writing mainly in English:

Muir, Edwin. COLLECTED POEMS, ed. by J. C. Hall and W. Muir. 2nd edn. *Faber* 1964, 25*s*.

Muir, Edwin. AN AUTOBIOGRAPHY. *Methuen* (*University Paperbacks*) 1965, 15*s*.

Muir, Edwin. THE ESTATE OF POETRY: the Charles Eliot Norton Lectures, 1955–56. *Hogarth Press* 1962, 18*s*.

For selective bibliography of Edwin Muir's separate volumes of verse, historical and critical writings, novels, etc., see J. C. Hall's EDWIN MUIR, *Longmans for the British Council* (*Writers and Their Work Series, No. 71*) 1956, 3*s* 6*d*. Among the critical studies of Muir are Helen L. Gardner's EDWIN MUIR, *Cardiff, University of Wales Press* (*The W. D. Thomas Lecture*) 1961, and Peter H. Butter's EDWIN MUIR, *Edinburgh, Oliver & Boyd* 1962, 7*s* 6*d*.

Other contemporary poets writing mainly in English are Norman A. McCaig, William Jeffrey, Ruthven Todd, George Sutherland Fraser, William Sydney Graham, James Findlay Hendry, Joseph Macleod ('Adam Drinan'), George Bruce, Hamish Henderson, Iain Crichton Smith, George Mackay Brown, Edwin Morgan, Stewart Conn, Alan Bold, Kenneth White and George Macbeth.

(b) *Fiction*

Mitchell, James Leslie ('Lewis Grassic Gibbon'). A SCOTS QUAIR.

Jarrolds 1966, 30*s*.

This trilogy comprises SUNSET SONG, 1932, CLOUD HOWE, 1933, and GREY GRANITE, 1934. For bibliography of Mitchell's works and of critical references to it, by G. Wagner, see *The Bibliotheck*, Vol. I, No. 1, 1956, and No. 2, 1957. See also Ian S. Munro's LEWIS GRASSIC GIBBON: a critical biography, *Edinburgh, Oliver & Boyd* 1966, 42*s*.

Gunn, Neil Miller.

See bibliography by W. R. Aitken in *The Bibliotheck*, Vol. III, No. 3, 1961. There is a critical work in Japanese by T. Nakamura entitled NEIL M. GUNN: a study, *University of Tokyo Press* 1962.

Linklater, Eric. The Orkney edition of THE WORKS OF ERIC LINKLATER, *Cape*, begun in 1950, is in progress.

Other Scottish novelists whose works are wholly or in part a contribution to the native Scots tradition are Sir Compton Mackenzie, George Blake, G. Scott-Moncrieff, Tom MacDonald ('Fionn MacColla'), Moray Maclaren, Naomi Mitchison, Fred Urquhart, Ian Macpherson, J. D. Scott, and Clifford Hanley.

VIII GAELIC

The common literary Gaelic, shared by Ireland and the Highlands, was the written language of books and manuscripts until well on in the seventeenth century. The great wealth of oral song and story in vernacular Scottish Gaelic, although rooted in an ancient tradition, was not recorded in writing until the later eighteenth century, as a consequence of the controversy over the authenticity of Macpherson's 'Ossianic' works. Traditionally, all poetry, whether anonymous or by known poets, was sung or chanted. This wealth of verse has been added to in every generation, and the subject matter reflects the changes in society and the poets' reactions to them. The last generation has also seen the emergence of a new thing—a school of poetry divorced from music, inspired both by the native tradition and by the literatures of other countries. Original prose, other than that of the oral tradition of tales—folk, heroic and historical—is no older than the nineteenth century, and first appeared in periodicals, notably those published by Dr Norman Macleod, and today in *Gairm*, a quarterly.

Bibliography

Maclean, Donald. TYPOGRAPHIA SCOTO-GADELICA: or books printed in the Gaelic of Scotland from 1567 to 1914. *Edinburgh, John Grant* 1915.

Dictionaries

Dwelly, Edward. THE ILLUSTRATED GAELIC–ENGLISH DICTIONARY. *Glasgow, Maclaren* 1949.

MacBain, Alexander. ETYMOLOGICAL DICTIONARY OF THE GAELIC LANGUAGE. *Stirling, Mackay* 1911.

MacLennan, Malcolm. A PRONOUNCING AND ETYMOLOGICAL DICTIONARY OF THE GAELIC LANGUAGE: Gaelic-English, English-Gaelic. *Edinburgh, John Grant* 1925.

Grammar

Calder, George. GAELIC GRAMMAR. *Glasgow, Maclaren* 1935.

Dialect Studies

Borgström, Carl H. THE DIALECT OF BARRA IN THE OUTER HEBRIDES. *Oslo, H. Ashehoug* 1937.

Borgström, Carl H. THE DIALECTS OF THE OUTER HEBRIDES. *Oslo, H. Ashehoug* 1940.

Borgström, Carl H. THE DIALECTS OF SKYE AND ROSS-SHIRE. *Oslo, H. Ashehoug* 1941.

Oftedal, Magne. THE GAELIC OF LEURBOST, ISLE OF LEWIS. *Oslo, H. Ashehoug* 1956.

This and the three preceding works are all parts of NORSK TIDSSKRIFT FOR SPROGVIDENSKAP.

Holmer, Nils. M. THE GAELIC OF ARRAN. *Dublin Institute of Advanced Studies* 1957.

Holmer, Nils M. THE GAELIC OF KINTYRE. *Dublin Institute of Advanced Studies* 1962.

Holmer, Nils M. STUDIES IN ARGYLLSHIRE GAELIC. *Upsala, Kungliga Humanistika Vetenskaps-Samfund* 1938, Skrifter 31:1.

Celtic Scholarship

Campbell, John Lorne and Thomson, Dericks. EDWARD LHUYD IN THE SCOTTISH HIGHLANDS, 1699–1700. *Oxford, Clarendon Press* 1963, 63*s*.

Lhuyd was the first to attempt a comparative study of the

Celtic languages. His notes made during his visit to the Highlands cover a very wide range of studies.

Skene, W. F. CELTIC SCOTLAND. 3 vols. *Edinburgh, David Douglas* 1886–90.

Skene, W. F. THE HIGHLANDERS OF SCOTLAND. 2nd edn. *Stirling, Mackay* 1902.

This edition of a work first published in 1836, has an excursus and notes by Dr Alexander MacBain which are a valuable corrective to some of Skene's views.

Cameron, Alexander. RELIQUIAE CELTICAE: texts, papers and studies in Gaelic literature and philology. 2 vols. *Inverness, Northern Chronicle Office* 1892–94.

Histories of Literature

Maclean, Magnus. THE LITERATURE OF THE HIGHLANDS. *Blackie* 1904.

MacNeill, Nigel. THE LITERATURE OF THE HIGHLANDERS. *Stirling, Mackay* 1929.

Texts of Manuscripts

Macfarlane, Malcolm, *ed.* LAMH-SGRIOBHAINN MHIC RATH. *Dundee, M. C. Macleod* 1924.

The Fernaig MS., a collection of verse compiled towards the end of the seventeenth century by Duncan Macrae, of Inverinate, in Kintail.

Quiggin, E. C., *ed.* POEMS FROM THE BOOK OF THE DEAN OF LISMORE. *Cambridge University Press* 1937.

An anthology in the Dean's peculiar orthography, of Gaelic poems, Irish and Scottish, including some as late as the early sixteenth century, composed in the literary language and in the versification of the bardic schools of the professional poets.

Ross, Neil, *ed.* HEROIC POETRY FROM THE BOOK OF THE DEAN OF LISMORE. *Edinburgh, Oliver & Boyd* 1939, 16*s*.

Here are good texts of the type of genuine 'Ossianic' poems made use of in his own peculiar way by James Macpherson.

Watson, W. J., *ed.* SCOTTISH VERSE FROM THE BOOK OF THE DEAN OF LISMORE. *Edinburgh, Oliver & Boyd* 1937.

Tales, Oral Traditions, etc.

Campbell, *Lord* Archibald and others. WAIFS AND STRAYS OF

CELTIC TRADITION. 5 vols. *Nutt* 1889–95.
Mostly folk and hero tales and clan traditions.

Campbell, *Lord* Archibald, *ed.* RECORDS OF ARGYLL. *Edinburgh, Blackwood* 1885.
A collection of popular history and clan traditions recorded in Argyll.

Campbell, J. Gregorson. SUPERSTITIONS OF THE HIGHLANDS AND ISLANDS OF SCOTLAND: collected entirely from oral sources. *Glasgow, Maclehose* 1900.

Campbell, J. Gregorson. WITCHCRAFT AND SECOND SIGHT IN THE HIGHLANDS AND ISLANDS OF SCOTLAND: tales and traditions collected entirely from oral sources. *Glasgow, Maclehose* 1902.
Both this and the above book present the material in English, with occasional Gaelic words and phrases in brackets.

Campbell of Islay, John F. LEABHAR NA FEINNE. *Spottiswoode for the author* 1872.
Heroic ballads, with variants, collected from MSS. and from oral tradition.

Campbell of Islay, John F., *comp. and ed.* POPULAR TALES OF THE WEST HIGHLANDS. 4 vols. *Paisley* 1890–93.
First edition 1860–62.

McKay, John G. MORE WEST HIGHLAND TALES, transcribed and trans. from the original Gaelic. 2 vols. *Edinburgh, Oliver & Boyd for the Scottish Anthropological and Folklore Society* 1940, 1960.
Tales taken from unpublished part of J. F. Campbell of Islay's collection.

Campbell, John Lorne, *ed. and trans.* STORIES FROM SOUTH UIST, told by Angus Maclellan. *Routledge & Kegan Paul* 1961, 30*s.*
Hero tales, simple folk tales, ghost stories, etc., forty-two in all.

MacKechnie, John, *ed.* THE DEWAR MANUSCRIPTS, Vol I: Scottish West Highland Folk Tales, collected by John Dewar for George Douglas, VIIIth Duke of Argyll, trans. into English by Hector Maclean of Islay; ed. with introd. and notes by J. MacKechnie. *Glasgow, Maclellan* 1964, 63*s.*

Proverbs

Nicolson, Alexander. GAELIC PROVERBS, collected and trans. into English. Reprinted by Malcolm MacInnes. *Glasgow, Caledonian Press* 1951.

Anthologies

Campbell, John Lorne. HIGHLAND SONGS OF THE FORTY-FIVE. *Edinburgh, John Grant* 1933.
With translations.

Carmichael, Alexander. CARMINA GADELICA. 5 vols. *Edinburgh, Oliver & Boyd* 1928–54.
Vols. I and II out of print; Vols. III and IV, 30*s* each; Vol. V, 36*s*.

Craig, K. C. ORAIN LUAIDH. *Glasgow, Alasdair Matheson* 1949.
A collection of 'waulking' songs.

MacDonald, Angus and MacDonald, Archibald. THE MACDONALD COLLECTION OF GAELIC POETRY. *Inverness, The Northern Counties Newspaper and Printing & Publishing Co.* 1911.
Miscellaneous Gaelic verse from area roughly that of former Lordship of the Isles. All previously unpublished; partly from manuscripts and partly from oral tradition.

Macdonald, Archibald. UIST BARDS. *Glasgow, Archibald Sinclair* 1894.

MacKenzie, John. THE BEAUTIES OF GAELIC POETRY. *Edinburgh, John Grant* 1907.
First published 1841. Poems mostly by known authors, with short biographies.

Macleod, Angus. SAR ORAIN: three Gaelic poems. *Glasgow, An Comunn Gaidhealach* 1933.
The longest poem of Mary MacLeod, Alexander MacDonald and Duncan Ban Macintyre respectively. Very fully annotated. Only adequate edition of MacDonald's famous poem on the Birlinn or Galley of Clan Ranald.

Sinclair, A. Maclean. THE GAELIC BARDS. 1411–1715; 1715–1765; 1775–1825; 1825–1875. 4 vols. *Charlottetown* 1890, 1892, *Sydney C.B.* 1896, 1904.
Published at the Mac-Talla Office.

Sinclair, A. Maclean. CLARSACH NA COILLE. *Glasgow, Maclaren* 1928.
First edn. 1881. A. M. Sinclair's publications incorporate verse orally preserved in Nova Scotia and they also draw on manuscripts taken to Nova Scotia by his grandfather.

Sinclair, Archibald. AN T-ORANAICHE. *Glasgow, Archibald Sinclair* 1879.
The most comprehensive published collection of popular Gaelic songs.

Sinton, Thomas. THE POETRY OF BADENOCH. *Inverness, Northern Chronicle Office* 1906.

With prose translations. Much previously unpublished. Represents eastern borders of Gaeldom. Covers several centuries.,

Watson, W. J., *ed.* BARDACHD GHAIDHLIG: specimens of Gaelic poetry, 1550–1900. 3rd edn. *Glasgow. An Comunn Gaidhealach* 1959, 17*s* 6*d*.

First published, Inverness 1918.

Individual Poets

Buchanan, Dugald. SPIRITUAL SONGS, ed. by Donald Maclean. *Edinburgh, John Grant* 1913.

The most notable Scottish Gaelic religious poet.

[Mackay], Rob Donn. SONGS AND POEMS, ed. by Hew Morrison. *Edinburgh, John Grant* 1899.

The eighteenth-century bard of the Reay country.

Hay, George Campbell. FUARAN SLEIBHE. *Glasgow, Maclellan* 1948.

With translations. A poet of the modern school.

MacDonald, Alexander. THE POEMS OF ALEXANDER MACDONALD, ed. by Angus MacDonald and Archibald MacDonald. *Inverness, The Northern Counties Newspaper and Printing & Publishing Co.* 1924.

The famous Jacobite poet of the '45.

MacCodrum, John. THE SONGS OF JOHN MACCODRUM, ed. by W. Matheson. *Edinburgh, Oliver & Boyd* 1938.

MacCodrum, *c.* 1700–1779, was bard to Sir James MacDonald of Sleat. The airs given in an appendix.

MacDonald, John. ORAIN IAIN LUIM: songs of John MacDonald, Bard of Keppoch, ed. by Annie Mackenzie. *Edinburgh, Oliver & Boyd for the Scottish Gaelic Texts Society* 1964, 42*s*.

Covers period from wars of Montrose to the Union of the Parliaments.

Macintyre, Duncan. THE SONGS OF DUNCAN BAN MACINTYRE, ed. by Angus MacLeod. *Edinburgh, Oliver & Boyd for the Scottish Gaelic Texts Society* 1952, 30*s*.

Duncan Ban, 1724–1812, the celebrated hunter bard of Glen Orchy.

Maclean, Sorley. DAIN DO EIMHIR. *Glasgow, Maclellan* 1943.

The outstanding Gaelic poet of his day and doyen of the modern school. With some translations.

MacLeod, Mary. GAELIC SONGS OF MARY MACLEOD, ed. by J. C. Watson. *Edinburgh, Oliver & Boyd for the Scottish Gaelic Texts Society* 1965, 21*s*.

The noted seventeenth-century poetess. With prose translation.

Ross, William. GAELIC SONGS . . . collected by John MacKenzie. New edn. rev. with metrical trans. etc. by George Calder. *Edinburgh Oliver & Boyd* 1937, 10*s* 6*d*.

Ross, 1763–1791, a lyrical poet of unrequited love.

Thomson, Derick S. AN DEALBH BRISTE. *Edinburgh, Serif Books* 1951. Poems in the modern manner, with some translations into English.

Prose

Watson, W. J., *ed.* ROSG GAIDHLIG: specimens of Gaelic prose. *Glasgow, An Comunn Gaidhealach* 1929.

First published Inverness 1915.

Thomson, R. L. *ed.* ADTIMCHIOL AN CHREIDIMH: the Gaelic version of John Calvin's Catechismus Ecclesiae Genevensis. *Edinburgh, Oliver & Boyd for the Scottish Gaelic Texts Society* 1962, 30*s*.

The translation is into the old literary Gaelic. First published *c.* 1631

MacLeod, J. N. LITRICHEAN ALASDAIR MHOIR. *Stornoway* 1932.

Selection from a series of Gaelic letters on various subjects contributed to the *Stornoway Gazette* 1917–32.

MacLeod, Norman. CARAID NAN GAIDHEAL. *Glasgow, William Mackenzie* 1867.

A selection by A. Clerk, of the prose works of this great master of modern Gaelic prose.

Lamont, Donald. PROSE WORKS OF DONALD LAMONT, 1874–1958, ed. by Thomas M. Murchison. *Edinburgh, Oliver & Boyd for the Scottish Gaelic Texts Society* 1960, 21*s*.

MacKinnon, Donald. PROSE WRITINGS OF DONALD MACKINNON, 1839–1914, ed. by Lachlan MacKinnon. *Edinburgh, Oliver & Boyd for the Scottish Gaelic Texts Society* 1956, 25*s*.

6 Philosophy

The wide international influence of Scottish philosophy, not only of Hume and Adam Smith, but also of their critics and successors such as Reid and Dugald Stewart, Brown and Hamilton, is such that a complete bibliography would have to draw heavily on American, French, Italian, German and other sources. However, quite a wide field is covered in:

Jessop, T. E. A BIBLIOGRAPHY OF DAVID HUME AND OF SCOTTISH PHILOSOPHY: from Francis Hutcheson to Lord Balfour. *A. Brown* 1938.

The best introduction and general background is found in a group of nineteenth-century French studies, including a contribution by Charles de Remusat in *Revue des deux Mondes*, April 1856, and the following:

Cousin, Victor. PHILOSOPHIE ECOSSAISE. 3rd. edn. *Paris, Librairie Nouvelle* 1857.
The 2nd edn. 1840, is virtually a different and less effective book.

Chasles, Victor E. Philarète. VOYAGE D'UN CRITIQUE A TRAVERS LA VIE ET LES LIVRES: l'Angleterre littéraire. 2 vols. *Paris, Librairie Nouvelle* 1876–78.

Boutroux, Emile. ETUDES D'HISTOIRE DE LA PHILOSOPHIE. 3rd edn. rev. *Paris* 1908.

In the 'study' entitled "De l'influence de la philosophie écossaise sur la philosophie française", Emile Boutroux discusses authoritatively, with documentation, the whole question of the Scottish influence on French philosophy.

Scottish studies are less balanced and complete, although indispensable; interpretations tend to be affected by polemical purposes regarding Scottish institutions, e.g.;

McCosh, J. THE SCOTTISH PHILOSOPHY: biographical, expository, critical, from Hutcheson to Hamilton. *Edinburgh, Macmillan* 1875.

Strongly evangelical and anti-establishmentarian.

Seth, Andrew (Pringle-Pattison). SCOTTISH PHILOSOPHY: a comparison of the Scottish and German answers to Hume. *Edinburgh,*

Blackwood (*Balfour Philosophical Lectures*) 1907.
Tries to promote united front with evangelicals against an irresponsible modernism.

Among the Scottish contributions, the biographies of the philosophers are the most notable:

Stewart, Dugald. BIOGRAPHICAL MEMOIRS OF ADAM SMITH, WILLIAM ROBERTSON, AND THOMAS REID. *Edinburgh, Cadell* 1811.
Gives ecclesiastical background to Scottish Enlightenment.

Welsh, David. ACCOUNT OF THE LIFE AND WRITINGS OF THOMAS BROWN. *Edinburgh, W. & C. Tait* 1825.

Veitch, John. MEMOIR OF SIR WILLIAM HAMILTON. *Edinburgh, Blackwood* 1869.

Haldane, Elizabeth S. JAMES FREDERICK FERRIER. *Edinburgh, Oliphant* (*Famous Scots Series*) 1899.

Jones, *Sir* Henry and Muirhead, J. H. THE LIFE AND PHILOSOPHY OF EDWARD CAIRD. *Glasgow, Maclehose* 1921.
Both this and the above title illustrate the long struggle between the epigoni of the Common Sense School and the Scottish Hegelians.

Stirling, Amelia Hutchison. JAMES HUTCHISON STIRLING: his life and work. *Unwin* 1912.
Devoted to Hegel but the foe of Anglo-Hegelianism.

Fraser, Alex. Campbell. BIOGRAPHIA PHILOSOPHICA: a retrospect. *Edinburgh, Blackwood* 1904
This autobiography of Ferrier's opponent represents the continuing Common Sense standpoint.

Wenley, R. M. See his very lively reminiscent essays in (a) Vol. II of CONTEMPORARY AMERICAN PHILOSOPHY, ed. by G. P. Adams and W. P. Montague, *Allen & Unwin* 1930, ("An Unborn Idealism") and (b) dispersed in fragments in Donald Macmillan's LIFE OF ROBERT FLINT, *Hodder & Stoughton* 1914.

The following are among the most important texts:

Hutcheson, Francis. AN INQUIRY INTO THE ORIGINAL OF OUR IDEAS OF BEAUTY AND VIRTUE. Published together with selections of other works by Hutcheson, 1694–1746, in Vol. I of BRITISH MORALISTS, ed. by Sir Lewis A. Selby-Bigge, *Oxford University Press* 1897.

Hume, David. THE PHILOSOPHICAL WORKS OF DAVID HUME, ed. by T. H. Green and T. H. Grose. 4 vols. *Longmans* 1875.

Hume, David. A TREATISE OF HUMAN NATURE. *Collins* (*Fontana*) 1962, 7*s* 6*d*; *Dent* (*Everyman's Library*) n.d., 2 vols. 8*s* 6*d* each.; *Oxford, Clarendon Press* 1897, 21*s*.

Hume, David. ENQUIRIES CONCERNING HUMAN UNDERSTANDING, ed. by Sir Lewis A. Selby-Bigge. 2nd edn. *Oxford, Clarendon Press* 1902, 20*s*.

Stewart, Dugald. THE COLLECTED PHILOSOPHICAL WORKS, ed. by Sir William Hamilton. 11 vols. *Edinburgh, Constable* 1877.

Reid, Thomas. PHILOSOPHICAL WORKS, ed. by Sir William Hamilton. 2 vols. *Edinburgh* 1895.

Brown, Thomas. INQUIRY INTO THE RELATION OF CAUSE AND EFFECT. *London* 1835.

An enlarged edition of OBSERVATIONS ON THE NATURE AND TENDENCY OF THE DOCTRINE OF MR HUME CONCERNING THE RELATION OF CAUSE AND EFFECT, *Edinburgh* 1805.

Brown, Thomas. LECTURES ON THE PHILOSOPHY OF THE HUMAN MIND, vol. 1. 20th edn. *William Tegg* 1860.

Hamilton, *Sir* William. LECTURES ON METAPHYSICS AND LOGIC. 4 vols. 3rd edn. *Edinburgh, Blackwood* 1865-74.

Mill, John Stuart. AN EXAMINATION OF SIR WILLIAM HAMILTON'S PHILOSOPHY. 6th edn. *Longmans* 1889.

Created a controversy which had world-wide repercussions.

Ferrier, James F. PHILOSOPHICAL WORKS. 3 vols. *Edinburgh, Blackwood* 1875.

Adamson, Robert, THE DEVELOPMENT OF MODERN PHILOSOPHY. *Edinburgh, Blackwood* 1903.

The following are important twentieth-century contributions to the study of Scottish philosophy:

On Hume

Greig, John Y. T. DAVID HUME. *Cape* 1931.

Greig, John Y. T., *ed.* THE LETTERS OF DAVID HUME. 2 vols. *Oxford University Press* 1932.

Mossner, E. C. THE LIFE OF DAVID HUME. *Nelson* 1954.

Klibansky, R. and Mossner, E. C. NEW LETTERS OF DAVID HUME. *Oxford University Press* 1954.

Hendel, C. W. STUDIES IN THE PHILOSOPHY OF DAVID HUME. 2nd. edn. *New York, Bobbs-Merril* 1963, cased $5.00; paper $2.95.

Maund, C. HUME'S THEORY OF KNOWLEDGE. *Macmillan* 1937.

Smith, N. Kemp. THE PHILOSOPHY OF DAVID HUME. *Macmillan* 1941, cased 45*s*; paper 21*s*.

Passmore, J. A. HUME'S INTENTIONS. *Cambridge University Press* 1952.

Bagolini, L. ESPERIENZA GIURIDICA E POLITICA NEL PENSIERO DI DAVID HUME. *Siena* (*Studi Senesi nel Circolo Giuridico della Università, Vol. LX*) 1947.

Stewart, John B. MORAL AND POLITICAL PHILOSOPHY OF DAVID HUME. *Columbia University Press* 1963, 56*s*.

Rotwein, Eugene, *ed.* WRITINGS ON ECONOMICS BY DAVID HUME. *Edinburgh, Nelson* 1955.

On Others

Cropsey, Joseph. POLITY AND ECONOMY. *Batsford* 1957.
An excellent general study of Adam Smith.

Bagolini, Luigi, LA SIMPATIA NELLA MORALE E NEL DIRITTO: aspetti del pensiero di Adam Smith. *Bologna, Cesare Zuffi* 1952.

Sciacca, M. F. LA FILOSOFIA DI TOMMASO REID CON UN APPENDICE SUI RAPPORTI CON GALLUPI E ROSMINI. *Naples* (*Biblioteca di Filosofia*) 1936.

Rasmussen, S. V. THE PHILOSOPHY OF SIR WILLIAM HAMILTON. *London, Hachette* 1925.

General

Sergerstedt, Torgny. THE PROBLEM OF KNOWLEDGE IN SCOTTISH PHILOSOPHY. *University of London Press* 1935.

Grave, S. A. THE SCOTTISH PHILOSOPHY OF COMMON SENSE. *Oxford, Clarendon Press* 1960, 38*s*.

Rhetoric

The books on rhetoric mentioned below are a part of Scottish philosophy and are only properly understood in relation to its characteristic procedures. The tradition of the intellectual treatment of rhetoric can be traced in its unbroken descent from Hugh Blair's LECTURES ON RHETORIC AND BELLES LETTERS, *W. Strahan and Cadell* 1783, George Campbell's very profound THE PHILOSOPHY OF RHETORIC. Rev. edn., *Edinburgh, Constable & Fairholm* 1816, not to mention Adam Smith's recently discovered lectures, through William Spalding's contributions to the 7th edn. of ENCYCLOPAEDIA BRITANNICA and Alexander Bain's ENGLISH COMPOSITION AND RHETORIC, enl. edn., *Longmans* 1887, to Sir Herbert Grierson's RHETORIC AND ENGLISH COMPOSITION. Rev. edn., *Edinburgh, Oliver & Boyd* 1951.

7 Education

I GENERAL

The Scottish educational system has developed over the years its own characteristic features and differs from that of England and Wales not only in terminology but in more material respects, such as the organisation of secondary education and the system of teacher training.

The evolution of Scottish education is described in the following works, which are mainly historical in treatment:

Kerr, J. SCOTTISH EDUCATION: school and university from early times to 1908. *Cambridge University Press* 1913.
With an addendum, 1908–13.

Grant. J. HISTORY OF THE BURGH SCHOOLS OF SCOTLAND. *Collins* 1876.

Strong, J. A. HISTORY OF SECONDARY EDUCATION IN SCOTLAND. *Oxford, Clarendon Press* 1909.

Edgar, J. HISTORY OF EARLY SCOTTISH EDUCATION. *Edinburgh, J. Thin* 1893.

Morgan, A. THE RISE AND PROGRESS OF SCOTTISH EDUCATION. *Gurney & Jackson* 1927.

Morgan, A. MAKERS OF SCOTTISH EDUCATION. *Longmans* 1929.
With bibliography.

Knox, H.M. TWO HUNDRED AND FIFTY YEARS OF SCOTTISH EDUCATION, 1696–1946. *Edinburgh, Oliver & Boyd* 1953, 18*s*.
Attention of legislative and administrative framework.

Saunders, L. J. SCOTTISH DEMOCRACY, 1815–1840. *Edinburgh, Oliver & Boyd* 1950, 21*s*.
For social and intellectual background.

For accounts of the development of Scottish education in recent years and for critical comment on current trends reference may be made to:

Mackintosh, M. EDUCATION IN SCOTLAND: yesterday and today. *Glasgow, Gibson*, 1962, 25*s*.

Osborne, G. S. SCOTTISH AND ENGLISH SCHOOLS: a comparative study of the past fifty years. *Longmans* 1966, 42*s*.

Kerr, A. J. C. SCHOOLS OF SCOTLAND. *Glasgow, Maclellan* 1962, 15*s*.

Mackenzie, R. F. A QUESTION OF LIVING. *Collins* 1963, 18*s*.

The publications of the *Scottish Council for Research in Education* (*London University Press*) deal with many aspects of education, e.g. EDUCATIONAL AND OTHER ASPECTS OF THE 1947 SCOTTISH MENTAL SURVEY, 1958.

Macpherson, J. S. ELEVEN-YEAR-OLDS GROW UP. 1958. 15*s*.

Boyd, W. EDUCATION IN AYRSHIRE THROUGH SEVEN CENTURIES. 1961, 20*s*.

Much detailed information will be found in the publications of the *Scottish Education Department.* Their booklet PUBLIC EDUCATION IN SCOTLAND, *H.M.S.O.*, 4*s*., which provides a general description of the educational system except for the Universities, contains a useful list of official publications. These include the Department's Annual Report, with statistics, EDUCATION IN SCOTLAND IN 1966, 8*s*; publications containing recommendations on various aspects of education, e.g. PRIMARY EDUCATION IN SCOTLAND, 1965, 10*s* 6*d*. and JUNIOR SECONDARY EDUCATION, 1955, 10*s* 6*d*; reports of committees, e.g. THE CURRICULUM OF THE SENIOR SECONDARY SCHOOL, 1959, 3*s* 6*d*, FROM SCHOOL TO FURTHER EDUCATION, 1963; and the reports of the *Advisory Council on Education in Scotland*, e.g. PRIMARY EDUCATION, 1946, 6*s*. (Cmd. 6973), SECONDARY EDUCATION, 1947 (Cmd. 7005), FURTHER EDUCATION, 1952 (Cmd. 8454), and TRANSFER FROM PRIMARY TO SECONDARY EDUCATION, 1961 (Cmnd. 1538), MEMORANDUM WITH REGARD TO THE PROVISION MADE FOR RELIGIOUS INSTRUCTION IN THE SCHOOLS OF SCOTLAND, 1943 (Cmd. 6426).

Law, Alexander. EDUCATION IN EDINBURGH IN THE 18TH CENTURY. *University of London Press* 1965.

Rea, F. G. A SCHOOL IN SOUTH UIST: reminiscences of a Hebridean school-master, 1890–1913, ed. by John Lorne Campbell. *Routledge & Kegan Paul* 1964, 30*s*.

II UNIVERSITIES

The distinctive features of the traditions and institutions of the old Universities of Scotland, three of them (St. Andrews, Glasgow and

Aberdeen) founded in the fifteenth century, the fourth (Edinburgh) in the late sixteenth, are derived from a history almost entirely independent of the English Universities. The three mediaeval foundations, all collegiate (though Glasgow and Aberdeen never had more than one college), were modelled on the northern Universities of the Continent, Paris, Cologne and Louvain, and maintained their essential character when they were reconstituted after the Reformation: Edinburgh (and the contemporary fifth foundation of Marischal College, Aberdeen, which was united with its older neighbour in 1860) followed the general pattern which was then established.

A. Morgan's SCOTTISH UNIVERSITY STUDIES, *Oxford University Press* 1933, provides a general survey of constitutional and academic development. G. E. Davie's THE DEMOCRATIC INTELLECT, *Edinburgh University Press* 1961, 50*s*, is a study of the intellectual life of the Universities in the nineteenth century. On the several Universities the following works may be consulted:

(a) HISTORY

St. Andrews

Cant, R. G. THE UNIVERSITY OF ST. ANDREWS. *Edinburgh, Oliver & Boyd* (*St. Andrews University Publications*) 1946.

Cant, R. G. THE COLLEGE OF ST. SALVATOR. *Edinburgh, Oliver & Boyd* (*St. Andrews University Publications, No. XLVII*) 1950, 15*s*.

Salmond. J. B. VETERUM LAUDES. *Edinburgh, Oliver & Boyd* (*St. Andrews University Publications, No. XLVIII*) 1950, 15*s*.

Glasgow

Mackie, J. D. THE UNIVERSITY OF GLASGOW, 1451–1951. *Glasgow, Jackson* 1951, 15*s*.

Murray, D. MEMORIES OF THE OLD COLLEGE OF GLASGOW. *Glasgow, Jackson* 1927.

FORTUNA DOMUS (Quincentenary Lectures on the Studies of the University). *Glasgow, Jackson* 1951, 15*s*.

Aberdeen

Rait, R. S. THE UNIVERSITIES OF ABERDEEN. *Aberdeen, J. G. Bisset* 1895.

Henderson, G. D. THE FOUNDING OF MARISCHAL COLLEGE. *Aberdeen University Press* 1947.

Simpson, W. Douglas. THE FUSION OF 1860: a record of the centenary celebrations and a history of the United University of Aberdeen, 1860–1960. *Edinburgh, Oliver & Boyd* (*Aberdeen University Studies, No.* 146) 1963, 20*s*.

Edinburgh

Grant, *Sir* Alexander. THE STORY OF THE UNIVERSITY OF EDINBURGH DURING THE FIRST 300 YEARS. *Longmans* 1884.

Turner, A. L. HISTORY OF THE UNIVERSITY OF EDINBURGH, 1883–1933. *Edinburgh, Oliver & Boyd* 1933.

Horn, David B. A SHORT HISTORY OF THE UNIVERSITY OF EDINBURGH, 1556–1889. *Edinburgh University Press* 1967, 45*s*.

(b) RECORDS AND DOCUMENTS

St. Andrews

Dunlop, A. I. ACTA FACULTATIS ARTIUM UNIVERSITATIS SANCTIANDREE, 1413–1588. *Edinburgh, Oliver & Boyd* (*St. Andrews University Publications, No. LVI*) 1964, 63*s*.

Anderson, J. M. EARLY RECORDS OF THE UNIVERSITY OF ST. ANDREWS, 1413–1579. *Edinburgh, Scottish History Society* 1926.

Anderson, J. M. MATRICULATION ROLL OF THE UNIVERSITY OF ST. ANDREWS, 1747–1897. *St. Andrews University* 1905, 12*s* 6*d*.

Glasgow

Innes, Cosmo. MUNIMENTA ALMAE UNIVERSITATIS GLASGUENSIS, 1451–1727. *Glasgow, Maitland Club* 1854.

Addison, W. I. ROLL OF GRADUATES OF THE UNIVERSITY OF GLASGOW, 1727–1897. *Glasgow, Maclehose* 1898.

Addison, W. I. THE MATRICULATION ALBUMS OF THE UNIVERSITY OF GLASGOW, 1728–1858. *Glasgow, Maclehose* 1913.

Aberdeen

Anderson, P. J. OFFICERS AND GRADUATES OF KING'S COLLEGE, 1495–1860. *Aberdeen, New Spalding Club* 1893.

Anderson, P. J., *ed.* FASTI ACADEMIAE MARISCALLANAE ABERDONENSIS: selections from the records of the Marischal College and University, 1593–1860. 3 vols. *Aberdeen, New Spalding Club* 1889–98.

Johnston, W. ROLL OF GRADUATES, 1860–1900. *Aberdeen University Press* 1906.

Watt, T. ROLL OF GRADUATES, 1900–1925. *Aberdeen University Press* 1935.

Edinburgh

Morgan, A. CHARTERS, STATUTES AND ACTS, 1583–1858. *Edinburgh, Oliver & Boyd* 1937.

Information about recent development may be found in the annual and quinquennial reports of the *University Grants Committee.*

8 Law

The main sources of Scots Law comprise statute law, case law, institutional treatises (which are accorded special authority) and legal treatises which have persuasive authority according to the reputation of their authors. The United Kingdom legislates today for Scotland, and Acts applicable to Scotland will be found in official collections, and in the unofficial series SCOTTISH CURRENT LAW STATUTES which is most usefully annotated. Some pre-Union (1707) legislation of the Scottish Parliament is still in force. Such legislation will be found in ACTS OF THE PARLIAMENTS OF SCOTLAND, 1424–1707, *H.M.S.O.* (*Statutory Publications*), 55*s.*

So far as case law is concerned, the modern series are SESSION CASES (official) and SCOTS LAW TIMES (unofficial). Both series include decisions of the House of Lords in Scottish civil appeals, and decisions of the supreme civil and criminal Courts in Scotland, i.e. the Court of Session and the High Court of Justiciary.

High authority is accorded to certain 'institutional writers' whose works are regarded like those of Grotius and Voet in Roman-Dutch law, or Pothier in France prior to the Napoleonic codification. Such works comprise:

Bankton, *Lord.* AN INSTITUTE OF THE LAWS OF SCOTLAND. 3 vols. *Edinburgh, R. Fleming* 1751–3.

Bell, G. J. COMMENTARIES ON THE LAW OF SCOTLAND. 7th edn. *Edinburgh, T. & T. Clark* 1870.

Bell, G. J. PRINCIPLES OF THE LAW OF SCOTLAND. 10th edn. *Edinburgh, T. & T. Clark* 1899.

Erskine, J. AN INSTITUTE OF THE LAW OF SCOTLAND. New edn. by J. B. Nicolson. *Edinburgh, Bell & Bradfute* 1871.

Erskine, J. PRINCIPLES OF THE LAW OF SCOTLAND. 21st edn. *Edinburgh, Green* 1911.

Stair, *Viscount.* THE INSTITUTES OF THE LAW OF SCOTLAND. *Edinburgh, Bell & Bradfute.*

The 1832 edn. with More's notes is most generally used.

Kames, *Lord.* PRINCIPLES OF EQUITY. New edn. *Edinburgh, Bell &*

Bradfute, 1825.
This new edn. of 1825 is generally used.

Hume, *Baron*. COMMENTARIES ON THE LAW OF SCOTLAND RESPECTING CRIMES. 4th edn. *Edinburgh, Bell & Bradfute* 1844.

Mackenzie, *Sir* George. THE LAWS AND CUSTOMS OF SCOTLAND IN MATTERS CRIMINAL. *Edinburgh, Heirs of Andrew Anderson for Andrew Symson* 1699.

For introductory general reading the following books may be consulted—the four former being for the general reader and the fifth specifically written for law students entering on University studies:

Gibb, A. D. A PREFACE TO SCOTS LAW. 4th edn. *Edinburgh, Green* 1964, 17*s* 6*d*.

Smith, T. B. BRITISH JUSTICE: the Scottish contribution. *Stevens* 1961, 27*s* 6*d*.

Cooper, Thomas M. (*Lord* Cooper of Culross). SELECTED PAPERS, 1922–1954, ed. by J. M. Cooper. *Edinburgh, Oliver & Boyd* 1957.

Cooper, Thomas M. (*Lord* Cooper of Culross). THE SCOTTISH LEGAL TRADITION. 3rd edn., rev. by M. C. Merton. *Edinburgh, Saltire Society* (*Saltire Pamphlets*) 1965, 2*s* 6*d*.

Walker, D. M. THE SCOTTISH LEGAL SYSTEM. 2nd edn. *Edinburgh, Green* 1963, 70*s*.

Bibliographies specifying reports and treatises which can most usefully be consulted on particular branches of the law are contained in Walker's book mentioned above and in T. B. Smith's referred to below. The following list comprises only modern general treatises:

BELL'S DICTIONARY AND DIGEST OF THE LAW OF SCOTLAND. 7th edn. by G. Watson. *Edinburgh, Bell & Bradfute* 1890.

ENCYCLOPAEDIA OF THE LAWS OF SCOTLAND. 16 vols. *Edinburgh, Green* 1926–35.
With supplements up to 1952.

Gibb, A. D. STUDENTS' GLOSSARY OF SCOTTISH LEGAL TERMS. *Edinburgh, Green* 1946, 10*s*.

Gibb, A. D. and Dalrymple, A. W. SCOTTISH JUDICIAL DICTIONARY. *Edinburgh, Green* 1946.

Gloag, W. M. and Henderson, R. C. INTRODUCTION TO THE LAW OF SCOTLAND. 6th edn. *Edinburgh, Green* 1956, £5.

Smith, T. B. A SHORT COMMENTARY ON THE LAW OF SCOTLAND. *Edinburgh, Green* 1962, £5 5*s*.

At present the *Scottish Universities Law Institute* is engaged in the restatement of the most important branches of Scots Law in up to sixteen treatises; the whole series is due to be published within ten years. Titles that have already appeared are:

Mitchell, J. D. B. CONSTITUTIONAL LAW. *Edinburgh, Green* 1964, 65*s*.

Walker, D. M. THE LAW OF DELICT IN SCOTLAND. 2 vols. *Edinburgh, Green* 1966, £12 12*s*.

Anton, A. E. PRIVATE INTERNATIONAL LAW. *Edinburgh, Green* 1967, £10.

Gordon, G. H. CRIMINAL LAW IN SCOTLAND. *Edinburgh, Green* 1967, £12 12*s*.

Paton, G. C. H. and Cameron, J. G. LAW OF LANDLORD AND TENANT IN SCOTLAND. *Edinburgh, Green* 1967, £10.

Selected topics of Scottish legal history are dealt with in the twenty-three volumes so far published by the *Stair Society* and available to members (whether individual or institutions). Vol. I: THE SOURCES AND LITERATURE OF SCOTS LAW, *Edinburgh* 1936, and Vol. XX: INTRODUCTION TO SCOTTISH LEGAL HISTORY, *Edinburgh* 1958, are of particular general interest.

In STUDIES CRITICAL AND COMPARATIVE, *Edinburgh, Green* 1962, T. B. Smith has sought to place Scots Law in its appropriate comparative setting in relation to the European civilian tradition—from which Scots Law is largely derived—and in relation to English Law by which the Scottish system has been influenced in modern times.

George Buchanan's famous DIALOGUS DE JURE REGNI APUD SCOTOS has recently been translated by Duncan H. McNeill, and published with his commentary under the title THE ART AND SCIENCE OF GOVERNMENT AMONG THE SCOTS, *Glasgow, Maclellan* 1964, 30*s*.

Mercantile Law is treated in J. A. Lillie's THE MERCANTILE LAW OF SCOTLAND, 6th edn. *Edinburgh, Green* 1965, 60*s*.

9 Administration

I GENERAL

Milne, *Sir* David. THE SCOTTISH OFFICE. *Allen & Unwin* 1957, 21*s*.

Thomson, M. A. THE SECRETARIES OF STATE, 1681–1782. *Oxford University Press* 1932.

Murray, C. de B. HOW SCOTLAND IS GOVERNED. *Edinburgh, Moray Press* 1938.

Shaw, J. E. LOCAL GOVERNMENT IN SCOTLAND, PAST, PRESENT AND FUTURE. *Edinburgh, Oliver & Boyd* 1942.

McLarty, M. R. A SOURCE BOOK AND HISTORY OF ADMINISTRATIVE LAW IN SCOTLAND. *Edinburgh, Hodge* 1946.

Miller, J. Bennett. OUTLINE OF ADMINISTRATIVE AND LOCAL GOVERNMENT LAW. *Edinburgh, Green* 1961, 60*s*.

Scottish Office. SCOTTISH ADMINISTRATION, A HANDBOOK. Rev. edn. *Edinburgh, H.M.S.O.* 1967, 8*s*

Scottish Home Department:

LOCAL GOVERNMENT IN SCOTLAND. *H.M.S.O.* 1958, 4*s*.

LOCAL GOVERNMENT AND CENTRAL DEPARTMENTS IN SCOTLAND. *H.M.S.O.* (*Cmnd. 445*) 1958, 9*d*.

LOCAL GOVERNMENT FINANCE IN SCOTLAND. *H.M.S.O.* (*Cmnd. 208*) 1957, 8*d*.

Scottish Development Department:

REORGANISATION OF LOCAL GOVERNMENT IN SCOTLAND: First Report. *H.M.S.O.* 1964, 1*s* 3*d*.

THE MODERNISATION OF LOCAL GOVERNMENT IN SCOTLAND: First Report. *H.M.S.O.* (*Cmnd. 2067*) 1964, 1*s* 3*d*.

Paton, H. J. THE CLAIM OF SCOTLAND. *Allen & Unwin* 1968, 42*s*.

II PUBLIC HEALTH: HEALTH SERVICES

There is no general study of public health and health services in Scotland. Recent historical surveys are:

Ferguson, T. THE DAWN OF SCOTTISH SOCIAL WELFARE. *Nelson* 1948.

Covering the period up to the mid-nineteenth century.

Ferguson, T. SCOTTISH SOCIAL WELFARE, 1864–1914. *Edinburgh, Livingstone* 1958, 42*s*.

Brotherston, J. H. F. OBSERVATIONS ON THE EARLY PUBLIC HEALTH MOVEMENT IN SCOTLAND. *H. K. Lewis* 1952, 21*s*.

On the special problems of a large city see:

Russell, J. B. PUBLIC HEALTH ADMINISTRATION IN GLASGOW. *Glasgow, Maclehose* 1905.

A memorial volume of the writings of an outstanding nineteenth-century medical officer of health.

Chalmers, A. K. THE HEALTH OF GLASGOW, 1818–1925. *Glasgow Corporation* 1930.

More recent developments are covered in:

Ross, J. Stirling. THE NATIONAL HEALTH SERVICE IN GREAT BRITAIN. *Oxford University Press* 1952.

Chapter 8 discusses Scottish antecedents of the National Health Service. Chapters 28–30 deal with the National Health Service in Scotland.

Central Office of Information. HEALTH SERVICES IN BRITAIN. Current edn. *H.M.S.O.* 5*s*.,

Contains a chapter on health services in Scotland.

Scottish Home and Health Department. NATIONAL HEALTH SERVICE, SCOTLAND. *H.M.S.O.* 1966, 20*s*.

For a contemporary record, see the long series of annual reports by the Scottish Home and Health Department and its predecessors:

1845–93: ANNUAL REPORTS OF THE GENERAL BOARD OF SUPERVISION.

1894–1919: ANNUAL REPORTS OF THE LOCAL GOVERNMENT BOARD FOR SCOTLAND.

1919–28: ANNUAL REPORTS OF THE SCOTTISH BOARD OF HEALTH.

1929–62: ANNUAL REPORTS OF THE DEPARTMENT OF HEALTH FOR SCOTLAND. For 1960 and 1961 the HEALTH AND WELFARE section of the report was published separately as Part II.

1963,64,66: HEALTH AND WELFARE SERVICES IN SCOTLAND. *Scottish Home and Health Department* 1966, 9*s*.

Since 1959 the reports have been supplemented by an annual volume of SCOTTISH HEALTH STATISTICS, 1965, 45*s*. Much interesting material is also contained in the annual reports of medical officers of health.

Landmarks in the development of Scottish Health Services are provided by a number of notable reports by official committees:

REPORTS ON THE SANITARY CONDITIONS OF THE LABOURING POOR OF GREAT BRITAIN: local reports relating to Scotland, 1842.

REPORT OF A DEPARTMENTAL COMMITTEE ON POOR LAW MEDICAL RELIEF IN SCOTLAND, 1904. *H.M.S.O.* (*Cd. 2008*).

REPORT ON THE HOSPITAL AND NURSING SERVICES IN SCOTLAND, 1920. *H.M.S.O.* (*Cmd. 699*).

REPORT OF THE (Cathcart) COMMITTEE ON SCOTTISH HEALTH SERVICES, 1936. *H.M.S.O.* (*Cmd. 5204*).

The special problems of the Highlands and Islands were surveyed in:

REPORT OF THE HIGHLANDS AND ISLANDS MEDICAL SERVICE COMMITTEE, 1912. *H.M.S.O.* (*Cd. 6559*).

Studies of the current problems of the National Health Service in Scotland are contained in a series of reports by the Scottish Health Services Council: for example, TUBERCULOSIS (1951), THE GENERAL PRACTITIONER AND THE HOSPITAL SERVICE (1952), MATERNITY SERVICES IN SCOTLAND (1959), MENTAL HEALTH SERVICES OF LOCAL AUTHORITIES (1961), and THE YOUNG CHRONIC SICK (1964). The work of the Council is summarized in their annual reports, published as an annex to the reports of the Department of Health for Scotland for 1949 to 1955, and independently since then.

On the history of Scottish Medicine, see:

Comrie, J. D. HISTORY OF SCOTTISH MEDICINE. *Wellcome Research Institution* 1927.

III HOUSING

Department of Health for Scotland. HOUSING SUBSIDIES IN SCOTLAND: report of the Working Party. *H.M.S.O.* 1956, 1*s*.

Department of Health for Scotland. HOUSING POLICY IN SCOTLAND. *H.M.S.O.* (*Cmd. 8997*) 1953, 6*d*.

Department of Health for Scotland. HOUSING IN SCOTLAND. *H.M.S.O.* (*Cmnd. 1520*) 1961, 1*s*.

Scottish Development Department. HOUSING RETURNS FOR SCOTLAND. *H.M.S.O.* (Quarterly).

Scottish Development Department. RENTS OF HOUSES OWNED BY LOCAL AUTHORITIES IN SCOTLAND. *H.M.S.O.* (Annually).

1962. *H.M.S.O.* (*Cmnd. 1923*) 1963, 2*s*.

1963. *H.M.S.O.* (*Cmnd. 2277*) 1964, 2*s*.

1964. *H.M.S.O.* (*Cmnd. 2598*) 1965, 2*s* 3*d*.

1965. *H.M.S.O.* (*Cmnd. 2907*) 1966, 2*s* 6*d*.

1966. *H.M.S.O.* (*Cmnd. 3194*) 1967, 2*s* 6*d*.

1967. *H.M.S.O.* (*Cmnd. 3523*) 1968, 2*s* 6*d*.

Scottish Building Costs Committee. INCREASE IN COST OF MAINTAINING HOUSES. *H.M.S.O.* 1953, 9*d*.

Department of Health for Scotland. REPORT OF THE COMMITTEE ON BUILDING LEGISLATION IN SCOTLAND. Chairman C. W. Graham Guest. *H.M.S.O.* (*Cmnd. 269*) 1957, 5*s* 6*d*.

Department of Health for Scotland. SCOTTISH HOUSING HANDBOOK.

Part I. Introduction: Housing Layout. *H.M.S.O.* 1958, 6*s*.

Part II. (See Scottish Development Department below.)

Part III. HOUSE DESIGN. *H.M.S.O.* 1956, 4*s* 6*d*.

Part IV. EQUIPMENT OF HOUSES. *H.M.S.O.* 1952, 6*d*.

Part V. TENDERS AND SPECIFICATIONS. *H.M.S.O.* 1955, 1*s* 6*d*.

Part VI. ECONOMY IN HOUSE BUILDING. *H.M.S.O.* 1952, 6*d*.

Part VII. HOUSING PROCEDURE FOR LOCAL AUTHORITIES. *H.M.S.O.* 1958, 3*s*.

Scottish Development Department. SCOTTISH HOUSING HANDBOOK 2: Roads and services. *H.M.S.O.* 1963, 3*s*.

Scottish Housing Advisory Committee. THE HOUSING OF SPECIAL GROUPS. *H.M.S.O.* 1952, 5*s*.

Scottish Housing Advisory Committee. DESIGN AND WORKMANSHIP OF NON-TRADITIONAL HOUSES. *H.M.S.O.* 1951, 1*s* 9*d*.

Department of Health for Scotland. SLUM CLEARANCES. *H.M.S.O.* (*Cmd. 9685*) 1956, 1*s*.

Scottish Development Department and Central Office of Information. IMPROVE YOUR HOUSE WITH A GRANT. *H.M.S.O.* 1963.

Scottish Development Department and the Scottish Housing Advisory Council. SCOTLAND'S OLDER HOUSES: Report by a sub-committee of the Scottish Housing Advisory Council. *H.M.S.O.* 1967, 10*s* 6*d*.

Scottish Development Department. BUILDING (SCOTLAND) ACT 1959 AND BUILDING STANDARDS (SCOTLAND) REGULATIONS 1963: explanatory memorandum. Administrative and General, including parts 1, 2, 7, 13, 14 and 16. [bound in one]. *H.M.S.O.* 1964, 3*s*.

Scottish Development Department. BUILDING STANDARDS (SCOTLAND) REGULATIONS 1963: explanatory memoranda. Parts 3, 4, 5, 6, 8, 9, 10, 11, 12 and 15. *H.M.S.O.* 1963–64. Various prices.

Scottish Development Department. MEMORANDUM ON THE DRAFT BUILDING STANDARDS (SCOTLAND) AMENDMENT REGULATIONS. *H.M.S.O.* 1965, 1*s* 6*d*.

Memoranda designed to be read in conjunction with STATUTORY INSTRUMENT 1963 No. 1897 (S. 102), BUILDING AND BUILDINGS: BUILDING STANDARDS (SCOTLAND) REGULATIONS 1963. *H.M.S.O.* 1963, 11*s*.

The following are reports of the Scottish Housing Advisory Committee:

RURAL HOUSING IN SCOTLAND. *H.M.S.O.* (*Cmd. 5462*) 1937, 1*s* 6*d*.

REHOUSING OF AGED PERSONS. *H.M.S.O.* (*Cmd. 5798*) 1938, 9*d*.

PLANNING OUR NEW HOMES. *H.M.S.O.* 1944, 3*s*.

DISTRIBUTION OF NEW HOUSES IN SCOTLAND. *H.M.S.O.* (*Cmd. 6552*) 1944, 2*s*.

THE PROVISION OF HOUSES FOR OWNER-OCCUPATION IN SCOTLAND. *H.M.S.O.* (*Cmd. 6741*) 1946, 1*s* 3*d*.

HOUSING MANAGEMENT IN SCOTLAND. *H.M.S.O.* (*Cmd. 6901*) 1946, 9*d*.

MODERNISING OUR HOMES. *H.M.S.O.* 1947, 2*s* 6*d*.

CHOOSING COUNCIL TENANTS. *H.M.S.O.* 1949.

Registrar-General for Scotland. ANNUAL REPORTS.

Ministry of Health and Department of Health for Scotland. REPORT OF THE INTER-DEPARTMENTAL COMMITTEE ON RENT CONTROL. *H.M.S.O.* (*Cmd. 6621*) 1945, 1*s*.

REPORT OF THE ROYAL COMMISSION ON THE HOUSING OF THE INDUSTRIAL POPULATION OF SCOTLAND, RURAL AND URBAN. *H.M.S.O.* (*Cd. 8731*) 1917.

Department of Health for Scotland. REPORT OF THE COMMITTEE ON SCOTTISH BUILDING COSTS. *H.M.S.O.* 1948, 1*s* 3*d*.

REPORT OF THE SCOTTISH DEPARTMENTAL COMMITTEE ON HOUSING. *H.M.S.O.* (*Cmd. 4469*) 1934, 1*s* 6*d*.

HOUSING. *H.M.S.O.* (*Cmnd. 2050*) 1963, 1*s* 3*d*.

Sub-Committee Scottish Advisory Council. HOUSING MANAGEMENT IN SCOTLAND. *H.M.S.O.* 1967, 9*s*. ALLOCATING COUNCIL HOUSES. *H.M.S.O.* 1967, 5*s* 6*d*.

REGISTRATION OF TITLE TO LAND IN SCOTLAND. *H.M.S.O.* (*Cmnd. 2032*) 1963, 3*s* 6*d*.

ORGANISATION AND PRACTICES FOR BUILDING AND CIVIL ENGINEERING. *H.M.S.O.* 1964.

Gordon, W. THE LAW OF HOUSING IN SCOTLAND. *Edinburgh, Hodge* 1952, 50*s*.

Bowley, Marion. HOUSING AND THE STATE. *Allen & Unwin* 1945.
See Appendix 1: Scottish Housing Problems.

Ballantine, W. M. REBUILDING A NATION. *Edinburgh, Oliver & Boyd* 1944.

Page, C. S. LOCAL FINANCE IN SCOTLAND. *Edinburgh, Hodge* 1961.

Cramond, R. D. ALLOCATION OF COUNCIL HOUSES. *Edinburgh, Oliver & Boyd* (*University of Glasgow Studies*) 1963, 6*s*.

IV TOWN AND COUNTRY PLANNING

Department of Health for Scotland. ANNUAL REPORTS PART II HOUSING, PLANNING AND ENVIRONMENT. *H.M.S.O.* (*Cmnd. 1703*) 1962, 4*s*.
Information in these reports is continued in the annual reports of the Scottish Development Department.

Scottish Development Department. ANNUAL REPORTS. *H.M.S.O.*

1962 (*Cmnd. 2004*), 8*s*.

1963 (*Cmnd. 2326*), 7*s*.

1964 (*Cmnd. 2635*), 9*s* 6*d*.

1965 (*Cmnd. 2948*), 9*s* 6*d.*

1966 (*Cmd. 3209*), 10*s* 6*d.*

1967 (*Cmd. 3553*), 11*s.*

Scottish Office. REVIEW OF HIGHLAND POLICY. *H.M.S.O.* (*Cmnd 785*) 1959, 9*d.*

Department of Health for Scotland. DEVELOPMENT PLANS: technical broadsheets 1 to 24. *H.M.S.O.* 1952, 7*s.*

Scottish Development Department. TECHNICAL BROADSHEET 26 SURVEYING AND PLANNING PROPOSALS FOR TOURISM. *H.M.S.O.* 1962, 5*s.*

Scottish Development Department. CIRCULAR 2, 1962 DEVELOPMENT PLANS (A) AREAS OF GREAT LANDSCAPE VALUE AND (B) TOURIST DEVELOPMENT PROPOSALS. *H.M.S.O.* 1962, 1*s.*

Scottish Development Department. CENTRAL SCOTLAND: a programme for development and growth. *H.M.S.O.* (*Cmnd. 2188*) 1963, 5*s.*

Scottish Office. DEVELOPMENT AND GROWTH IN SCOTLAND, 1963–64. *H.M.S.O.* (*Cmnd. 2440*) 1964, 3*s* 6*d.*

Cumbernauld, East Kilbride, Glenrothes and Livingston Development Corporations ANNUAL REPORTS.

1962. *H.M.S.O.* 1962, 10*s.*

1963. *H.M.S.O.* 1963, 12*s.*

1964. *H.M.S.O.* 1964, 12*s.*

1965. *H.M.S.O.* 1965, 15*s.*

1966. *H.M.S.O.* 1966, 16*s* 6*d.*

1967. *H.M.S.O.* 1967, 17*s* 6*d.*

Department of Scientific and Industrial Research. REGIONAL GEOLOGY STUDIES. *H.M.S.O.*

British Association for the Advancement of Science. SCIENTIFIC SURVEY OF SOUTH-EASTERN SCOTLAND. *British Association* 1951.

British Association for the Advancement of Science. THE GLASGOW REGION: a general survey. *Ronald Miller & Joy Tivy* 1958.

British Association for the Advancement of Science. THE ABERDEEN REGION. *British Association* 1963.

Payne, G. THE TAY VALLEY PLAN. *Dundee, East Central (Scotland) Regional Planning Advisory Committee* 1950.

Scottish Development Department. LOTHIANS REGIONAL SURVEY PLAN, Vol. I: Economic and Social Aspects; Vol. II: Physical Planning Aspects. *H.M.S.O.* 1966, 75*s*. each (bound).

Water Resources Board and Scottish Development Department. REPORT ON 'SOLWAY BARRAGE'. *H.M.S.O.* 1967, 16*s*.

Scottish Development Department. WATER SERVICE IN SCOTLAND: final report of the Scottish Water Advisory Committee. *H.M.S.O.* (*Cmnd. 3116*) 1966, 8*s*.

Grimble, Ian and Thomson, Derick S. THE FUTURE OF THE HIGHLANDS. *Routledge & Kegan Paul* 1968, 45*s*.

10 Agriculture, Industry and Commerce

I AGRICULTURE

As an introduction to the development of Scottish agriculture the general reader will find interest in the books already mentioned under the sub-heading (c. 1) Agriculture in the HISTORY section on page 22. More specialized studies might well begin with the comprehensive, though not specifically Scottish, work:

Watson, J. A. S. and More, J. A. AGRICULTURE: the science and practice of British farming. *Edinburgh, Oliver & Boyd* 1962, 30*s*.

For the study of livestock production, which is the predominant feature of Scottish farming:

Fraser, Allan. SHEEP FARMING. 7th edn. *Crosby Lockwood* 1965, 12*s* 6*d*.

Fraser, Allan. FARMING FOR BEEF. 2nd edn. *Crosby Lockwood* 1950.

Fraser, Allan and Stamp, John T. SHEEP HUSBANDRY AND DISEASES. 4th edn. *Crosby Lockwood* 1961, 35*s*.

Marson, T. B. THE SCOTCH SHORTHORN. *Edinburgh, Scottish Shorthorn Breeders' Association* 1946.

Detailed studies on agricultural practice in Scotland are to be found in the following reports:

Stamp, L. Dudley, *ed.* THE LAND OF BRITAIN: THE REPORT OF THE LAND UTILISATION SURVEY OF BRITAIN. Thirty parts at various prices. Each part is published by *Geographical Publications for the Land Utilization Survey* 1937–46. Particulars of the parts are as follows:

Vol. I.

Lebon, John H. G. AYRSHIRE. Part 1. 1937.

Green, F. H. W. MORAY AND NAIRN. Part 2. 1937.

Smith, Frank T. SUTHERLAND. Part 3. 1939.

O'Dell, A. C. ORKNEY. Part 4. 1939.

O'Dell, A. C. ZETLAND. Part 5. 1940.

Dobson, E. B. BANFFSHIRE. Part 6. 1941.

Hare, F. Kenneth. KIRKCUDBRIGHT, WIGTOWN. Combined Parts 7 and 8. 1942, 4*s*.

Vince, S. W. E. THE HIGHLANDS OF SCOTLAND. Hunt, C. J. THE MAINLAND OF INVERNESS. Stamp, L. Dudley. BUTESHIRE. Combined Parts 10, 11, 12, 13. 1944.

Vol. II.

Waite, P. C. BERWICKSHIRE. Part 14. 1941.

Vince, S. W. E. CAITHNESS. Part 15. 1944, 4*s*.

Scola, P. M. THE LOTHIANS. Combined Parts 16, 17, 18. 1944, 4*s*.

McIver, J. A. DUMFRIESSHIRE. Part 19. 1945, 4*s*.

Moyes, Morag D. RENFREWSHIRE. Stamp. L. Dudley. LANARKSHIRE, DUNBARTONSHIRE, STIRLINGSHIRE. Combined Parts 20, 21, 22, 23. 1946, 4*s*.

Linton, David L. and Snodgrass, Catherine P. PEEBLESSHIRE, SELKIRKSHIRE. O'Dell, A. C. ROXBURGHSHIRE. Combined Parts 24, 25, 26. 1946, 4*s*.

Dobson, E. B. ANGUS. Stamp, L. Dudley. KINCARDINESHIRE. Ogg, W. G. and Muir, A. ABERDEENSHIRE. O'Dell, A. C., Snodgrass, Catherine P. and Stamp, L. Dudley. FIFE with KINROSS and CLACKMANNAN. Combined Parts 27, 28, 29, 30. 1946. 10*s*.

References to crofting agriculture are to be found elsewhere in this bibliography, but special mention might be made of the following:

Darling, F. Fraser. CROFTING AGRICULTURE. *Edinburgh, Oliver & Boyd* 1945.

Mackenzie, David. FARMER IN THE WESTERN ISLES. *Faber* 1954.

The history, development and researches in animal and human nutrition are dealt with in:

Cuthbertson, *Sir* David P., *ed.* PROGRESS IN NUTRITION AND ALLIED SCIENCES: being a contribution marking the first 50 years of the Rowett Research Institute. *Edinburgh, Oliver & Boyd for the Rowett Research Institute* 1963, 50*s*.

(a) GOVERNMENT PUBLICATIONS

The Department of Agriculture and Fisheries for Scotland SECTIONAL LIST (*H.M.S.O.*) contains a full list of Government publications in print including advisory leaflets and bulletins on technical subjects.

Department of Agriculture and Fisheries for Scotland. REPORT OF THE DEPARTMENT OF AGRICULTURE AND FISHERIES FOR SCOTLAND (*H.M.S.O. Annual*).

Department of Agriculture and Fisheries for Scotland. AGRICULTURAL STATISTICS: SCOTLAND (*H.M.S.O.* 1912 to date).

Department of Agriculture and Fisheries for Scotland. TYPES OF FARMING IN SCOTLAND (*H.M.S.O.* 1952).

ANNUAL REVIEW AND DETERMINATION OF GUARANTEES (*H.M.S.O. Annual*)—a joint publication with the Ministry of Agriculture, Fisheries and Food—announces the results of the annual review of the agricultural industry.

ANIMAL HEALTH SERVICES IN GREAT BRITAIN REPORT, including REPORT OF PROCEEDINGS UNDER THE DISEASES OF ANIMALS ACT 1950 (*H.M.S.O.* 1959, 6*s*)—published jointly with the Ministry of Agriculture, Fisheries and Food.

Department of Agriculture and Fisheries for Scotland. SCOTTISH AGRICULTURAL ECONOMICS, in Vols. I-XIV. (*H.M.S.O.*) Some studies of Current Economic Conditions in Scottish Farming.

Agricultural Research Council: Soil Survey Research Board. SOIL SURVEY OF GREAT BRITAIN REPORTS (Includes Soil Survey of Scotland (*H.M.S.O.* 1950 to date).

Department of Agriculture and Fisheries for Scotland. SCOTTISH AGRICULTURE (*H.M.S.O. Quarterly*, 1*s* 3*d*)—journal for farmers giving information with a scientific slant on new developments and techniques.

Consumers Committees for Great Britain and for Scotland REPORTS 1958—(*Ministry of Agriculture, Fisheries and Food* 1958 to date).

Joint publication of Ministry of Agriculture, Fisheries and Food and Home Office (reports on the operation of statutory marketing schemes under the Agricultural Marketing Act).

POTATO TRIALS AND COLLECTIONS AT EAST CRAIGS (*H.M.S.O.* 1962, 3*s* 6*d*)—key to trials carried out at the Department of Agriculture's Scientific Service Station at East Craigs, Edinburgh. REGISTER OF POTATO CROPS CERTIFIED (*H.M.S.O.* 1961, 6*s* 6*d*). RESIDUAL VALUES OF FERTILIZERS AND FEEDING-STUFFS (*H.M.S.O. Annual*).

Reports of the Scottish Standing Committee. FOWL PEST POLICY (*H.M.S.O.* 1962, 7*s*)—Committee Report.

Department of Agriculture for Scotland. HILL SHEEP FARMING IN SCOTLAND (*H.M.S.O. Cmd. 6704.* 1944, 2*s*)—a committee report.

Department of Agriculture for Scotland. HILL FARM RESEARCH REPORTS OF THE SCOTTISH HILL FARM RESEARCH COMMITTEE (*H.M.S.O.* 1951 and 1953).

Highland matters, particularly crofting are dealt with in the following:

CROFTING CONDITIONS. New edn. *H.M.S.O.* 1958, 5*s* 6*d.*
Report of Commission of Enquiry.

Hill Lands (North of Scotland) Commission. COMMITTEE REPORT. *H.M.S.O.* (*Cmd 9759*) 1955, 1*s* 3*d.*

PROGRAMME OF HIGHLAND DEVELOPMENT. *H.M.S.O.* 1951, 1*s* 9*d.*

REVIEW OF HIGHLAND POLICY. *H.M.S.O.* 1959, 9*d.*

CROFTERS COMMISSION REPORTS. *H.M.S.O.* Annual, 4*s.*

RED DEER COMMISSION REPORTS. *H.M.S.O.* Annual, 1*s* 9*d.*

Department of Agriculture and Fisheries for Scotland. LAND USE IN THE HIGHLANDS AND ISLANDS. *H.M.S.O.* 1964, 10*s.*

(b) EDUCATION, ADVISORY SERVICES AND RESEARCH

There are three Scottish Agricultural Colleges (providing a free advisory service for farmers as well as education to diploma standard) and ten Agricultural Research Institutes in Scotland. These bodies publish regular accounts of their work which are obtainable from the institution concerned.

II INDUSTRY AND COMMERCE

Scottish Statistical Office. DIGEST OF SCOTTISH STATISTICS. *H.M.S.O.* twice a year, 5*s* and 7*s* 6*d.*

Scottish Development Department. INDUSTRY AND EMPLOYMENT IN SCOTLAND. *H.M.S.O.* Annually 1947 to 1962/63.

ANNUAL REVIEW OF MAIN DEVELOPMENTS AND TRENDS IN ECONOMIC AFFAIRS, INCLUDING ROADS, IN SCOTLAND, the first, *H.M.S.O.* (*Cmd. 7125*) 1947, to fifteenth, *H.M.S.O.* (*Cmnd. 1391*) 1961, comp. by Scottish Home Department, the sixteenth, *H.M.S.O.* (*Cmnd. 1727*) 1962, and the seventeenth and last of the title, *H.M.S.O.* (*Cmnd. 2045*) 1963, 3*s*, by Scottish Development Department.

Scottish Development Department. ELECTRICITY IN SCOTLAND: report of the Committee on the generation and distribution of electricity in Scotland. Chairman C. H. Mackenzie. *H.M.S.O.* (*Cmnd. 1859*) 1962, 8*s* 6*d*.

North of Scotland Hydro-Electric Board. ANNUAL REPORTS AND ACCOUNTS INCLUDING REPORTS OF THE ELECTRICITY CONSULTATIVE COUNCIL FOR THE NORTH OF SCOTLAND DISTRICT. *H.M.S.O.* 5*s* and 7*s* 6*d*.

Scottish Development Department. HYDRO-ELECTRIC SCHEMES. REPORT OF THE PUBLIC ENQUIRY INTO THE NORTH OF SCOTLAND HYDRO-ELECTRIC BOARD'S CONSTRUCTIONAL SCHEME NO. 39 (FADA/FIONN PROJECT) AND CONSTRUCTIONAL SCHEME NO. 38 (LAIDON PROJECT). *H.M.S.O.* 1965, 9*s* 6*d*.

South of Scotland Electricity Board. ANNUAL REPORTS AND ACCOUNTS INCLUDING THE REPORTS OF THE ELECTRICITY CONSULTATIVE COUNCIL FOR THE SOUTH OF SCOTLAND DISTRICT. *H.M.S.O.* 5*s* 6*d* to 8*s*.

Scottish Development Department. THE WATER SERVICE IN CENTRAL SCOTLAND, REPORT OF THE SCOTTISH WATER ADVISORY COMMITTEE. Chairman Craig Mitchell. *H.M.S.O.* 1963, 7*s* 6*d*.

Oakley, C. A. SCOTTISH INDUSTRY. *Edinburgh, Scottish Council* (*Development and Industry*) 1953.

Scottish Television Ltd. SCOTLAND—THE VITAL MARKET: a survey of Scotland's economy. *Glasgow, Scottish Television* 1966 (private circulation).

Gaskin, Maxwell. THE SCOTTISH BANKS: a modern survey. *Allen & Unwin* (*University of Glasgow Social and Economic Studies, No. 6*). 1965, 36*s*.

11 Food and Drink

I FOOD

Scottish cookery has aptly been described as 'a pastoral cooking, brightly influenced by old ties with France'. A few of our traditional recipes are traceable to Old Holyrood, and many Franco-Scottish domestic terms are still in common use, but unfortunately none of our printed cookery-books goes further back than the middle of the eighteenth century. The most notable are:

Cleland, *Mrs* Elizabeth. A NEW AND EASY METHOD OF COOKERY. *Edinburgh, C. Wright* 1759.

Robertson, *Mrs* Hannah. THE YOUNG LADIES' SCHOOL OF ARTS. 2nd edn. *Edinburgh, printed for the author by Walter Ruddiman* 1767.

McIver, *Mrs* Susanna. COOKERY AND PASTRY. *Edinburgh* 1773.

Frazer, *Mrs* THE PRACTICE OF COOKERY. *Edinburgh* 1791.

In the early nineteenth century, before the whole business of brewing and distilling, pickling and preserving, was transferred from the stillroom to the factory, Scottish housewifery reached its zenith. By far the most outstanding book of this period is Meg Dods's THE COOK AND HOUSEWIFE'S MANUAL, *Edinburgh* 1826. Meg Dods is the *nom de plume* of Mrs Johnston, a contemporary and friend of Sir Walter Scott, and the humorous introduction to the book, which links it with St. Ronan's Well, is almost certainly written by Scott himself. The work contains over twelve hundred recipes collected from all over the British Isles and many Continental countries, and has a special section, 'Scottish National Dishes', containing some sixty recipes. Although it appeared more than thirty years earlier, it is of much wider range than Mrs Beeton's classic and contains, moreover, much amusing and informative material.

Another popular book of this period is Mrs Dalgairns's THE PRACTICE OF COOKERY, *Edinburgh, Cadell* 1829.

Of the cookery-books that appeared in the latter half of the nineteenth century, two that enjoyed wide popularity are 'Jenny

Wren', i.e. James Bertram, MODERN DOMESTIC COOKERY, *Paisley* 1880, and THE PRACTICE OF COOKERY AND PASTRY by Mrs Williamson of D. Williamson and Son, well-known Edinburgh cooks and caterers, *Edinburgh* 1862.

Although practically all the cookery-books published by Scots in the present century have more or less a Scottish accent, only a few are consciously concerned with the Scottish culinary tradition. These include:

Kitchin, A. H. and Passmore, R. THE SCOTSMAN'S FOOD: an historical introduction to modern food administration. *Edinburgh, Livingstone* 1949.

MacClure, Victor. SCOTLAND'S INNER MAN: a history of Scots food and cookery. *Routledge & Kegan Paul* 1935.

McNeill, F. Marian. THE SCOTS KITCHEN: its traditions and lore, with old-time recipes. New edn. *Glasgow, Blackie* 1963, 21*s*.

McNeill, F. Marian. RECIPES FROM SCOTLAND. *Edinburgh, Albyn Press* 1963, 9*s* 6*d*.

Morrison, John. A BOWL O' BROSE: national dishes from Scotland. *Glasgow, Celtic Art Society* 1947.

SCOTTISH WOMEN'S RURAL INSTITUTES COOKERY BOOK. *Edinburgh, S.W.R.I.* 1947.

Stout, Margaret. THE SHETLAND COOKERY BOOK. *Lerwick, Manson* 1965.

Craig, Elizabeth. THE SCOTTISH COOKERY BOOK. *André Deutsch* 1956, 21*s*.

II DRINK

These books all belong to the present century.

Bruce-Lockhart, *Sir* Robert. SCOTCH: the whisky of Scotland in fact and story. 3rd edn. *Putnam* 1966, 21*s*.

Gunn, Neil M. WHISKY AND SCOTLAND: a practical and spiritual survey. *Routledge* 1935.
Now a collector's piece.

Macdonald, Aeneas. WHISKY. *Faber* 1930.

McNeill, F. Marian. THE SCOTS CELLAR: its traditions and lore, with recipes. *Edinburgh, Paterson* 1956.

Wilson, Ross. SCOTCH MADE EASY. *Hutchinson* 1959.

Gillett, S. W. ILLICIT SCOTCH. *Aberdeen, Beaver Books* 1965, 18*s*.

12 Sport

I CRICKET

Aitchison, Rev. James. KILMARNOCK CRICKET CLUB: ONE HUNDRED —NOT OUT. *Kilmarnock Cricket Club* 1952.

Anderson, William. SELKIRK CRICKET CLUB CENTENARY, 1851–1951. *Galashiels, A. Walker* 1954.

Bone, D. D. FIFTY YEARS' REMINISCENCE OF SCOTTISH CRICKET. *Glasgow, Aird & Coghill* 1898.

Courtney, S. AS CENTURIES BLEND: one hundred and six years of Clydesdale Cricket Club. *Glasgow, John Miller* 1954.

Donaldson, *Rev.* H. C. AYR CRICKET CLUB, 1859–1959. '*Ayr Advertiser*' 1961.

O'Neil, Alfred. ANNALS OF BRECHIN CRICKET, 1849–1927. *Brechin, Black & Johnston* 1928.

Riddell, T. C. GREENOCK CRICKET CLUB RECORDS, 1887–1937. *Greenock, James McKelvie* 1938.

Stevenson, N. L. PLAY! The story of the Carlton Cricket Club and a personal record of over fifty years' Scottish cricket. *Edinburgh, C. J. Cousland* 1946.

II CURLING

Kerr, John. HISTORY OF CURLING. *Edinburgh, D. Douglas* 1890.

Ramsay, *Rev.* James. AN ACCOUNT OF THE GAME OF CURLING. *Edinburgh* 1882.

The author belonged to the Duddingston Curling Society.

Taylor, James. CURLING. *Edinburgh, W. Paterson* 1884.

III FISHING

'Black Palmer'. SCOTCH LOCH FISHING. *Edinburgh, Blackwood* 1882.

Blakey, Robert. THE ANGLER'S GUIDE TO THE RIVERS AND LOCHS OF SCOTLAND. *David Bogue* 1854.

Briggs, E. E. ANGLING AND ART IN SCOTLAND. *Longmans* 1908.

Castle, P. WHERE TO FISH IN SCOTLAND. *Edinburgh, Oliver & Boyd* 1931.

Hardie, R. P. FEROX AND CHAR IN THE LOCHS OF SCOTLAND: an inquiry, Part I. *Edinburgh, Oliver & Boyd* 1940.

Henzell, H. P. THE ART AND CRAFT OF LOCH FISHING. *Philip Allan* 1937.

Lamond, Henry. DAYS AND WAYS OF A SCOTTISH ANGLER. *Philip Allan* 1932.

Lamond, Henry. LOCH LOMOND. *Glasgow, Jackson, Wylie* 1931, 7*s* 6*d*.

Lawrie, William H. BORDER RIVER ANGLING. 2nd edn. *Edinburgh, Oliver & Boyd* 1959, 10*s* 6*d*.

Lawrie, William H. SCOTTISH TROUT FLIES: an analysis and a compendium. *Muller* 1966, 30*s*.

Leitch, A. A SCOTTISH FLY-FISHER. *Paisley, A. Gardner* 1911.

Robertson, R. Macdonald. IN SCOTLAND WITH A FISHING ROD. *Jenkins* 1935.

Robertson, R. Macdonald. IN SCOTLAND WITH A FISHING ROD. *Edinburgh, William Hodge* 1933.

Stewart, Charles. THE LAW OF FISHING. *Edinburgh, T. & T. Clark* 1892.
A treatise by an advocate on the law of Scotland relating to the rights of fishing.

Stewart, Tom. THE LOCHS OF SCOTLAND AND HOW TO FISH THEM. *Benn for the 'Angling Times'* 1964, 5*s*.

Stoddart, T. THE ANGLER'S COMPANION TO THE RIVERS AND LOCHS OF SCOTLAND, ed. by Sir Herbert Maxwell, *Jenkins* 1922.

IV FOOTBALL

Allison, William. RANGERS: the new era. *Glasgow, Rangers F.C.* 1966, 25*s*.

Fairgrieve, John. THE RANGERS. *Hale* 1964.
A complete history of the Club.

Handley, James E. THE CELTIC STORY. *Stanley Paul* 1960.

Mackay, Dave. SOCCER MY SPUR. *Stanley Paul* 1961.

Mackie, Albert David. THE HEARTS: a history of the Club. *Stanley Paul* 1959.

Maley, W. THE STORY OF THE CELTIC. *Glasgow, printed for the author* 1939.

Paterson, Tom. THE HISTORY OF THE HAWICK RUGBY FOOTBALL CLUB, 1873–1956. *Hawick, Scott & Paterson* 1956.

Phillips, R. J. THE STORY OF SCOTTISH RUGBY. *Foulis* 1925.

Reid, William. STORY OF 'THE HEARTS'; a fifty years retrospect, 1874–1924. *Edinburgh, Heart of Midlothian F.C.* 1924.

Young, George. CAPTAIN OF SCOTLAND. *Stanley Paul* 1951.

V GOLF

Clark, Robert, *ed.* GOLF: a royal and ancient game. 2nd edn. *Macmillan* 1893.

Everard, H. S. C. A HISTORY OF THE ROYAL AND ANCIENT GOLF CLUB ST. ANDREWS FROM 1754 TO 1900. *Edinburgh, Blackwood* 1907.

Kirkcaldy, Andra (of St. Andrews). FIFTY YEARS OF GOLF: my memories. *T. Fisher Unwin* 1921.

Reid, William. GOLFING REMINISCENCES, 1887–1925: the growth of the game. *Edinburgh, J. & J. Gray* 1935.

Robbie, J. Cameron. THE CHRONICLE OF THE ROYAL BURGESS GOLFING SOCIETY OF EDINBURGH, 1735–1935. *Edinburgh, Morrison & Gibb* 1936.

Salmond, J. B. THE STORY OF THE R. & A.: history of the first 200 years of the Royal and Ancient Golf Club of St. Andrews. *Macmillan* 1956.

VI LAWN TENNIS

ASPECTS OF SCOTTISH LAWN TENNIS. *Edinburgh, E. & S. Livingstone* 1910.

A series of articles.

Macgregor, A. Wallace. FIFTY YEARS OF LAWN TENNIS IN SCOTLAND. *Edinburgh, Scottish Lawn Tennis Association* 1927.

VII MOUNTAINEERING

Abraham, A. P. ROCK CLIMBING IN SKYE. *Longmans* 1908.

Baker, E. A. THE HIGHLANDS WITH ROPE AND RUCKSACK. *Witherby* 1923.

Bell, J. H. B. PROGRESS IN MOUNTAINEERING. *Edinburgh, Oliver & Boyd* 1950.

Humble, B. H. CUILLIN OF SKYE. *Hale* 1952.

Murray, W. H. MOUNTAINEERING IN SCOTLAND. New edn. *Dent* 1962, cased 25*s*; 1966, paper 8*s* 6*d*.

Murray, W. H. UNDISCOVERED SCOTLAND. *Dent* 1951.

Poucher, W. A. THE NORTH WEST HIGHLANDS. *'Country Life'* 1954.

Poucher, W. A. THE SCOTTISH PEAKS. *Constable* 1964, 25*s*.

Pyatt, E. C. MOUNTAINS OF BRITAIN. *Batsford* 1966, 25*s*.

CLIMBERS' GUIDES. *The Scottish Mountaineering Club* (*dist. Edinburgh, W. & R. Chambers*).

CLIMBERS' GUIDE TO BEN NEVIS. 1954.

CLIMBERS' GUIDE TO THE CAIRNGORM AREA. 2 vol. 1961. 1961, 62, 20*s* per vol.

CLIMBERS' GUIDE TO GLENCOE AND ARDGOUR. 2nd ed. 2 vol. 1959, 20*s* per vol.

CUILLIN OF SKYE ROCK CLIMBERS' GUIDE. 20*s*.

ROCK CLIMBS IN ARRAN. 1963, 20*s*.

SCOTTISH MOUNTAINEERING CLUB GUIDES. *The Scottish Mountaineering Club* (*dist. Edinburgh, W. & R. Chambers*).

BEN NEVIS. 1936.

THE CAIRNGORMS. 3rd edn. 1950.

THE CENTRAL HIGHLANDS. 2nd edn. 1952.

ISLAND OF SKYE. 2nd edn. 1948.

THE ISLANDS OF SCOTLAND (excluding Skye). 2nd edn. 1952, 25*s*.

THE NORTHERN HIGHLANDS. 3rd edn. 1953.

THE SOUTHERN HIGHLANDS. 1949, 25*s*.

THE WESTERN HIGHLANDS. 4th edn. 1964, 25*s*.

MUNRO'S TABLES OF THE 3000 FEET MOUNTAINS OF SCOTLAND AND OTHER TABLES OF LESSER HEIGHTS. *The Scottish Mountaineering Club (dist. Edinburgh, W. & R. Chambers)* 1953, 10*s* 6*d*.

VIII SHINTY

Macdonald, J. Ninian. SHINTY. *Inverness, Carruthers* 1932.
Foreword by Lord Lovat. The history of the game, with some illustrations of shinty in bygone days reproduced from old pictures.

IX SKI-ING

Firsoff, Valdemar A. ON SKI IN THE CAIRNGORMS. *Edinburgh, W. & R. Chambers* 1965, 10*s* 6*d*.

X STALKING, ETC.

Anderson, T. Scott. HOUND AND HORN IN JEDFOREST. *Jedburgh, T. S. Smail* 1909.

Cameron, Allan Gordon. THE WILD RED DEER OF SCOTLAND. *Edinburgh, Blackwood* 1923.

Chalmers, Patrick R. FIELD SPORTS OF SCOTLAND. *Philip Allan, now A. & C. Black (The Sportsman's Library)* 1936.

Latymer, *Lord*. STALKING IN SCOTLAND AND NEW ZEALAND. *Edinburgh, Blackwood* 1935.

Mackie, Peter Jeffrey. THE KEEPER'S BOOK. *G. T. Foulis* 1929.

McConnochie, Alexander Inkson. THE DEER AND DEERFORESTS OF SCOTLAND: historical, descriptive, sporting. *Witherby* 1923.

McConnochie, Alexander Inkson. DEER FOREST LIFE. *Glasgow, Maclehose* 1932.

McConnochie, Alexander Inkson. DEER STALKING IN SCOTLAND. *Witherby* 1923.

Peel, C. V. A. WILD SPORT IN THE OUTER HEBRIDES. *F. E. Robinson* 1901.

Pilkington, Stephen M. WITH A GUN TO THE HILL: THIRTY YEARS OF SPORT IN THE SCOTTISH HIGHLANDS. *Jenkins* 1948.

Portland, *Duke of*. FIFTY YEARS AND MORE OF SPORT IN SCOTLAND. *Faber* 1933.

Speedy, Tom. THE NATURAL HISTORY OF SPORT IN SCOTLAND WITH ROD AND GUN. *Edinburgh, Blackwood* 1920.

Stephens, Martin. GROUSE SHOOTING. *Philip Allan, now A. & C. Black (The Sportsman's Library)* 1939.

APPENDIX

THE HIGHLANDS AND ISLANDS OF SCOTLAND. *National Book League* 1967, 3*s*. A Bibliography.

Linklater, Eric. THE SURVIVAL OF SCOTLAND: a review of Scottish history. *Heinemann* 1968, 50*s*.

Chambers, R. TRADITIONS OF EDINBURGH. *Edinburgh, Chambers* 1967, 45*s*.

Moncreiffe of that Ilk, *Sir* Iain. THE HIGHLAND CLANS. *Barrie & Rockliff* 1967, 63*s*.

HISTORY OF THE FREE PRESBYTERIAN CHURCH OF SCOTLAND. Compiled by a Committee appointed by the Synod of the . . . Church. New edn. *Inverness, Free Presbyterian Church* 1965, 10*s* 6*d*.

Anderson, Mark L. A HISTORY OF SCOTTISH FORESTRY. 2 vols. *Nelson* 1967, £12 12*s*.

Lindsay, Jean. THE CANALS OF SCOTLAND. *Newton Abbot, David & Charles* 1968, 50*s*.

Marwick, W. H. A SHORT HISTORY OF LABOUR IN SCOTLAND. *Edinburgh, W. & R. Chambers* 1967, 15*s*.

Wilson, Gloria. SCOTTISH FISHING CRAFT. *Fishing News* 1965, 25*s*.

Wilson, Gloria. MORE SCOTTISH FISHING CRAFT. *Fishing News* 1968, 45*s*.

Jackson, W. T. THE ENTERPRISING SCOT: Investors in the American West after 1873. *Edinburgh University Press* 1968, 63*s*.

Sinclair-Stevenson, Christopher. THE GORDON HIGHLANDERS. *Hamish Hamilton* (*Famous Regiments Series*) 1968, 21*s*.

Howard, Philip. THE BLACK WATCH. *Hamish Hamilton* (*Famous Regiments Series*) 1968, 25*s*.

Other vols. to follow will include THE SCOTS GUARDS (25*s*) and THE HIGHLAND LIGHT INFANTRY (25*s*).

GUIDE TO SCOTLAND. New edn. *Edinburgh, W. & R. Chambers* 1967, 45*s*.

Cluness, A. T., *ed.* THE SHETLAND BOOK. *Lerwick, Zetland Education Committee* 1967, 25*s*.

Douglas, Hugh. PORTRAIT OF THE BURNS COUNTRY (and Galloway). *Hale* 1968, 25*s*.

Dymock, Eric. SCOTLAND BY CAR. *Newton Abbot, David & Charles* 1968, 25*s*.

Gaskell, Philip. MORVERN TRANSFORMED: a Highland parish in the nineteenth century. *Cambridge University Press* 1968, 65*s*.

Lochhead, Marion. PORTRAIT OF THE SCOTT COUNTRY. *Hale* 1968, 25*s*.

Simpson, W. Douglas. PORTRAIT OF SKYE AND THE OUTER ISLES. *Hale* 1967, 25*s*.

Swire, Otta F. THE OUTER HEBRIDES AND THEIR LEGENDS. *Edinburgh, Oliver & Boyd* 1966, 30*s*.

Swire, Otta F. SKYE, THE ISLAND AND ITS LEGENDS. Latest edn. with amendments. *Blackie* 1967, 22*s* 6*d*.

Wyness, Fenton. ROYAL VALLEY: the story of the Aberdeenshire Dee. *Aberdeen, Alex. P. Reid* 1968, 55*s*.

Forman, Sheila. SCOTTISH COUNTRY HOUSE AND CASTLE. *Collins* 1967, 30*s*.

Mackintosh, Charles Rennie. ARCHITECTURAL JOTTINGS. Selected by Andrew McLaren Young. *The Glasgow Institute of Architects* 1968, 7*s* 6*d*.

Cursiter, Stanley. PEPLOE. *Nelson* 1947.

Gillies, W. G. and Maxwell, John. AN EXHIBITION OF PAINTINGS, WATERCOLOURS AND DRAWINGS BY W. G. GILLIES AND JOHN MAXWELL. *The Arts Council of Great Britain* 1954.

Gordon, T. Crouther. DAVID ALLAN, OF ALLOA, 1744–1796: the Scottish Hogarth. *Alva, Robert Cunningham* 1951.

Honeyman, T. J. INTRODUCING LESLIE HUNTER. *Faber* 1937.

Bronson, B. H. THE TRADITIONAL TUNES OF THE CHILD BALLADS WITH THEIR TEXTS. Vol. 1–3. *Princeton University Press* (and *Oxford University Press* 1959–1966, £10 each.

In the Series 'Writers and their Work', published for the *British Council* and *the National Book League* by *Longmans, Green & Co.*, have appeared, in addition to those already listed in this book, the following booklets (critical studies with bibliographies) of Scottish authors:

TWO SCOTS CHAUCERIANS (Henryson and Dunbar), by H. Harvey Wood.

BOSWELL, by P. A. W. Collins.

HUME, by Montgomery Belgion.

FERRIER AND GALT, by W. M. Parker.

COMPTON MACKENZIE, by Kenneth Young.

Douglas, Gavin. THE SHORTER POEMS, ed. by Priscilla J. Bawcutt. *Edinburgh, Scottish Text Society* 1967, 63*s*.

Burns, Robert. THE POEMS AND SONGS OF ROBERT BURNS, ed. by James Kinsley. 3 vols. *Oxford University Press* 1968, £9 10*s*.

Smith, Janet Adam. JOHN BUCHAN: a biography. *Hart-Davis* 1965.

Smith, Janet Adam. R. L. STEVENSON. *Duckworth* (*Great Lives Series*) 1937.
Bruce, George, *ed.* THE SCOTTISH LITERARY REVIVAL: an anthology of twentieth-century poetry. *Collier Macmillan* 1968, 18*s*.
Lindsay, Maurice, *ed.* MODERN SCOTTISH POETRY: an anthology of the Scottish Renaissance. 2nd edn. *Faber* 1966, 21*s*.
Macintyre, Donald, 'The Paisley Bard'. SPORAN DHÒMHNAILL: Gaelic Poems and Songs. Compiled and edited by Somerled Macmillan. *Edinburgh, Oliver & Boyd for the Scottish Texts Society* 1968, 35*s*.
Ferguson, Adam. AN ESSAY ON THE HISTORY OF CIVIL SOCIETY 1767, *ed.* Duncan Forbes. *Edinburgh University Press* 1966, 42*s*.
Steuart, *Sir* James. AN INQUIRY INTO THE PRINCIPLES OF POLITICAL ŒCONOMY, ed. Andrew Skinner. 2 vols. *Edinburgh, Oliver & Boyd* 1966, £7.
Young, Douglas; Youngson, A. J. *and others*. EDINBURGH IN THE AGE OF REASON: a commemoration. *Edinburgh University Press* 1967, 10*s* 6*d*.
Bone, Thomas R., *ed.* STUDIES IN THE HISTORY OF SCOTTISH EDUCATION, 1872–1939. *University of London Press* 1967, 37*s*. 6*d*. (Scottish Council for Research in Education Publications, 54).
Coissac, J. B. LES UNIVERSITÉS D'ÉCOSSE DEPUIS LA FONDATION DE L'UNIVERSITÉ DE ST. ANDREWS JUSQU'AU TRIOMPHE DE LA RÉFORME (1410–1560). *Paris, Larousse* 1915.
Osborne, G. S. CHANGE IN SCOTTISH EDUCATION. *Longmans* 1968, 18*s*.
McDowall, R. J. S. THE WHISKIES OF SCOTLAND. *John Murray* 1968, 18*s*.
Robertson, John. UPPIES & DOONIES: the story of the Kirkwall Ba' Game. *Aberdeen University Press* 1967, 30*s*.
Emmerson, George S. SCOTLAND THROUGH HER COUNTRY DANCES. *Johnson* 1967, 35*s*.
Scottish Official Board of Highland Dancing. HIGHLAND DANCING. New edn. *Nelson* 1968, 30*s*.
Campbell, John Lorne, GAELIC IN SCOTTISH EDUCATION AND LIFE. 2nd edn. rev. *Edinburgh, W. & A. K. Johnston for the Saltire Society*, 1950, 3*s* 6*d*.

INDEX OF PERSONAL NAMES